Property of
INSTITUTE FOR WORSHIP STUDIES
Orange Park, Florida

The NORMAL CHRISTIAN CHURCH LIFE

WATCHMAN NEE

Living Stream Ministry
Anaheim, California • www.lsm.org

© 1980 Living Stream Ministry

All rights reserved. No part of this work may be reproduced or transmitted in any form or by any means—graphic, electronic, or mechanical, including photocopying, recording, or information storage and retrieval systems—without written permission from the publisher.

First Edition, July 1980.
Second Edition, August 1994.

ISBN 0-87083-027-9

Published by

Living Stream Ministry
2431 W. La Palma Ave., Anaheim, CA 92801 U.S.A.
P. O. Box 2121, Anaheim, CA 92814 U.S.A.

Printed in the United States of America

03 04 05 / 11 10 9 8 7 6 5

CONTENTS

Title	Page
Preface	v
Preface to the English Edition	vii
Introduction	ix
1 The Apostles	1
2 The Separation and Movements of the Apostles	19
3 The Elders Appointed by the Apostles	39
4 The Churches Founded by the Apostles	51
5 The Basis of Union and Division	73
6 The Work and the Churches	99
7 Among the Workers	119
8 The Question of Finance	139
9 The Organization of Local Churches	163

PREFACE

The contents of this book, with the exception of some minor adjustments to British punctuation, expressions, idioms, and spellings, have been taken directly from the edition published by Watchman Nee in England in 1939 under the title *Concerning Our Missions*. The 1939 English edition presents Watchman Nee's own work in the English language; he was directly responsible for its translation and editing. Any differences between the English and Chinese editions reflect Watchman Nee's own revisions.

PREFACE TO THE ENGLISH EDITION

After the publication of my book in Chinese, quite a number of missionaries asked for an English edition. I felt reluctant to comply, for personally I should prefer to have those books translated which better represent my ministry, rather than this one which is liable to be misunderstood and controverted. But that it was the Lord's mind seemed to be quite clear, and in that confidence I proceeded with the translation. The book as it now stands is a greatly abridged and slightly revised edition of the Chinese. Neither in expression nor in style is it as English as I should wish, but I trust that in this respect I may count on the leniency of its readers. If all we want is the truth of God, then the difficulty of understanding the book should prove no serious barrier to the reading of it.

Because of the vastness of the subject and the importance of its issues, I have not found it easy either to write or translate the book. Since some of the same points have had to be dealt with in different parts of the book, it will be found necessary to read it right through if full understanding is to result. If, because of seemingly insurmountable difficulty, the book is laid aside before being completed, a false position will result; whereas, by reading it right through, many, if not all, of the difficulties will be cleared up. Frequently the questions which arise at certain points are answered further on—sometimes much further on. So to do the book justice, the reader is asked to finish reading it before passing judgment.

The book is not intended for anyone and everyone. It is for those who bear responsibility in the Lord's service. But, more than this, it is for such as honestly and truly mean business with God, for those whose hearts are open and have no padlocked mind or prejudices. The book may test one's sincerity and honesty to no small degree; but genuine hunger and desire to know the Lord's full thought will sustain a careful reading to the end. I fully realize the many imperfections of this book (this is not a gesture, but a confession); but despite them all, I believe the Lord has shown something which is of importance to the whole Body of Christ.

The whole matter will grow upon the reader and become clearer with relaxed contemplation after the first reading. The door must not be closed with a snap of "Impossible!" or, "Ideal, but not practical!" By prayerful openness of heart, without argument or discussion, the Spirit of Truth should be given a chance, and then *what is of Him* will cause all our natural reactions to die away, and we shall know the truth and the truth shall make us free!

May I remind my readers that the book is not intended to be studied in a hypothetical way. I have quite a large number of fellow workers who have been sent out and are working along the lines indicated, and there are a larger number of churches which have been formed and developed on the basis mentioned.[1] So what is set forth in these pages is no mere theory or teaching, but something we have actually tested out.

One of the prayers I have offered in connection with this book is that the Lord should keep it from those who oppose and would use it as a chart for attack, and also from those who agree and would use it as a manual for service. I dread the latter far more than the former.

London
April 1939
W. Nee

---

[1] See Introduction.

INTRODUCTION

IMPORTANT TO UNDERSTANDING OF THE BOOK

The content of the following pages is the substance of a number of talks to my younger fellow workers during conferences held recently in Shanghai and Hankow. When the addresses were given, the present book was not in view, but only my immediate audience; and the fact that the messages were intended for the instruction of my young colleagues accounts for their intensely practical nature, and for the simplicity of the style adopted. At these two conferences we sought in the first place to examine the teaching of God's Word concerning His churches and His work, and in the second place to review our past missions in the light of our findings.[1]

The talks proved of value to my younger brethren, and, as longhand notes were taken, the messages were shared with others. This resulted in many requests that the addresses be put into book form. As the conferences were attended chiefly by my younger fellow workers, I felt at liberty to instruct and counsel them, and to discuss quite freely a number of intimate and rather delicate matters. Had the addresses been intended for a wider audience, or for publication, I should have felt obliged to omit many matters that were mentioned, and to speak in an altogether different strain. I naturally hesitated when the suggestion was made to publish them, but the Lord made it clear that that was His mind, so I have no option but to acquiesce. I questioned the wisdom of preserving the original style of the addresses, with their bits of "elder-brotherly" counsel and their distinct personal strain; but as a number of friends testified to special help received through the more

---

[1] The word "we" is used throughout this book as among fellow workers, for it was so used by the apostles in the book of Acts.

personal parts, I realized that the book would lose its greatest value if those were eliminated. Therefore, though I send the addresses forth somewhat revised, they still remain, both in matter and style, very much as they were when originally delivered.

We trust the readers of this book will bear in mind that its messages, as originally given, were never meant for them. They were intended exclusively for the inner circle of my most intimate associates in the work, but by request we share our findings with the wider circle of all our brethren. The book is something private made public; something originally intended for the few now extended to the many; so we trust our readers will pardon anything that seems unsuited to the wider public.

We should like to point out here the place of the teachings of this book in the great body of divine truth, for the former have spiritual value only as they are held in relation to the latter. During the past eighteen years, the Lord has led us through different experiences in order that we might learn a little of the principle as well as the fact of the cross and resurrection, and learn something of the Christ-life, the lordship of Jesus, the corporate life of the Body, the ground of the kingdom of God, and His eternal purpose. It is natural, therefore, that these things have been the burden of our ministry. But God's wine must have a wineskin to contain it. In the divine pattern, nothing is left for man to decide. God Himself has provided the best wineskin for His wine, which will contain and preserve it without loss, hindrance, or misrepresentation. He has shown us His wine, but He has shown us His wineskin also.

Our work, throughout the past years, has been according to certain definite principles; but never until now have we tried to define or teach them. We have sought rather, in the power of the Spirit, to stress those truths which are so dear to our hearts and which, we believe, have more direct bearing on the spiritual life of the believer and the eternal purpose of God. But the practical outworking of those truths in the Lord's service is by no means unimportant. Without that, everything is in the realm of theory, and spiritual development is impossible. So we would seek, by the grace of God, not only to pass on His good wine, but also the wineskin He has provided for its preservation. The truths set forth in this book must therefore be regarded in relation to those taught throughout the eighteen years of our ministry, and as the sequence, not the introduction, to them.

Within the scope of these pages, it has been impossible to deal with all the questions relating to the subject of the book. Some I have already dealt with elsewhere, and others I hope to deal with at a later date. *The title of the book explains its nature.* It is not a treatise on missionary methods, but a *review* of our past work in the light of God's will as we have discovered it in His Word. The Lord had most graciously led us by His Spirit in our past service for Him, but we wanted to be clear as to the foundations upon which all divine work should rest. I realized that the primary need of my younger brethren was to be led of the Spirit and to receive revelation from Him, but I could not ignore their need of a solid *scriptural* basis for all their ministry. Therefore, together we talked freely of what we had been doing and how we had been doing it, and sought to compare our work and methods with what God had set before us in His Word. We examined the scriptural reasons for the means we employed, and the scriptural justification for the end we pursued; and we made a note of various lessons we had learned by observation as well as by experience. There was no thought of criticizing the labors of others, or even of making any suggestion to them how the work of God ought to be conducted; we were merely seeking to learn from God's Word, from experience, and from observation, how to conduct the work in the days to come, so that we might be workmen "approved to God."

The book is written from the standpoint of a servant looking from the work *towards the churches*. It does not deal with the specific ministry to which we believe the Lord has called us, but only with the general principles of the work; nor does it deal with "the church, which is His Body," but with the local churches and their relation to the work. The book does not touch the principles of the work, or the life of the churches; it is only a review of our missions, as the title suggests.

The truths referred to in this book have been gradually learned and practiced during the past years. Numerous adjustments have been made as greater light has been received, and if we remain humble, and God still shows us mercy, we believe there will be further adjustments in the future. The Lord has graciously given us a number of associates in the work, all of whom have been sent forth on the basis mentioned in this book, and through their labors numerous churches have been established in different parts of China. Though conditions are vastly different in these many churches, and the believers connected with them differ greatly too—in background, education, social standing, and spiritual experience—yet we have found that if, under the absolute lordship of Jesus, we come to see the heavenly pattern of church formation and government, then the scriptural methods are both practicable and fruitful.

While the book itself may seem to deal with the technical side of Christianity, let us emphasize here that we are not aiming at mere technical correctness. It is spiritual reality we are after. But spirituality is not a matter of theory; it always issues in practice; and it is with spirituality in its practical out-working that this book deals.

It is wearisome to me, if not actually repulsive, to talk with those who aim at perfect outward correctness, while they care little for that which is vital and spiritual. Missionary methods, as such, do not interest me at all. In fact, it is a deep grief to meet children of God who know practically nothing of the hatefulness of a life lived in the natural energy of man, and know little of vital experience of the headship of Jesus Christ, yet all the while are scrupulously careful to arrive at absolute correctness of method in God's service. Many a time we have been told, "We agree with you in everything." Far from it! In reality we do not agree at all! We hope this book will not fall into the hands of those who wish to improve their work by improving their methods, without adjusting their relationship to the Lord; but we do hope it will have a message for the humble ones who have learned to live in the power of the Spirit and have no confidence in the flesh.

It is death to have a wineskin without wine, but it is loss to have wine without a wineskin. We must have the wineskin *after* we have the wine. Paul wrote the Ephesian Epistle, but he could also write the Corinthian Epistle; and Corinthians presents us with Ephesian truths in practical expression. Yes, the writer of Ephesians was also the writer of Corinthians! But why is it that the children of God have never had any serious contentions over Ephesian truths, but always over Corinthian truths? Because the sphere of Ephesians is the heavenlies, and its truths are purely spiritual, so if there is any diversity of opinion concerning them, no one feels it much; but Corinthian teachings are practical and touch the earthly sphere, so if there is the slightest difference of opinion, a reaction is felt at once. Yes, Corinthians is very practical! And it tests our obedience more than does Ephesians!

The danger, with those who know little about life and reality, is to emphasize mere outward correctness; but with those to whom life and reality are a matter of supreme importance, the temptation is to throw away the divine pattern of things, thinking it legal and technical. They feel that they have the greater and can therefore well dispense with the lesser. As a result, the more spiritual a man is, the freer he feels to do as he thinks fit. He considers that he himself has authority to decide on outward matters, and rather fancies that to ignore God's commands regarding them is an indication that he has been delivered from legality and is walking in the liberty of the Spirit. But God has not only revealed the truths that concern our inner life; He has also revealed the truths relating to the outward expression of that life. God prizes the inner reality, but He does not ignore its outward expression. God has given us Ephesians, Romans, and Colossians, but He has also given us Acts, the Epistles to Timothy, and the Epistles to the Corinthians. We may think it sufficient for God to instruct us through Romans, Ephesians, and Colossians as to our life in Christ, but He has considered it necessary to instruct us through Acts, Corinthians, and Timothy, how to do His work and how to organize His Church. God has left nothing to human imagination or human will. Man is afraid to use a thoughtless servant, but God does not care to use an over-thoughtful one; all He requires of man is simple obedience. "Who has become His counselor?" asked Paul (Rom. 11:34). Man would fain occupy the post, but God has no need of a counselor. It is not our place to suggest how we think divine work should be done, but rather to ask in everything, "What is the will of the Lord?"

The Pharisees cleansed the outside of the platter, but left the inside full of impurity. Our Lord rebuked them for setting so much store on outward things, and ignoring the inward; and many of God's people conclude from the Lord's rebuke that, providing we stress the inner side of spiritual truth, all is well. But God demands both inward and outward purity. To have the outer without the inner is spiritual death, but to have the inner without the outer is only spiritualized life. And spiritualization is not spirituality. Our Lord said, "These you should have done and not neglected the others" (Matt. 23:23). No matter how insignificant any divine command may seem, it is an expression of the will of God; therefore, we never dare treat it lightly. We cannot neglect the least of His commands with impunity. The importance of His requirements may vary, but everything that is of God has eternal purpose and eternal worth. Of course, the mere observance of outward forms of service has no spiritual value whatever. All spiritual truths, whether pertaining to the inner or the outer life, are liable to be legalized. Everything that is of God—whether outward or inward—if in the Spirit is life; if in the letter it is death. So the question is not whether it is outward or inward, but whether it is in the Spirit or in the letter. "The letter kills, but the Spirit gives life" (2 Cor. 3:6).

It is our desire to accept and proclaim the whole Word of God. We covet to be able to say with Paul, "I did not shrink from declaring to you all the counsel of God" (Acts 20:27). We seek to follow the leading of God's Spirit, but at the same time we seek to pay attention to the examples shown us in His Word. The leading of the Spirit is precious, but if there is no example in the Word, then it is easy to substitute our fallible thoughts and unfounded feelings for the Spirit's leading, drifting into error without realizing it. If one is not prepared to obey God's will in every direction, it is easy to do things contrary to His Word and still fancy one is being led of His Spirit. We emphasize the necessity of following both the leading of the Spirit and the examples of the Word, because by comparing our ways with the written Word we can discover the source of our leading. The Spirit's guidance will always harmonize with the Scriptures. God cannot lead a man one way in Acts and another way today. In externalities the leading may vary, but in principle it is always the same; for God's will is eternal, therefore changeless. God is the eternal God; He takes no cognizance of time, and His will and ways all bear the stamp of eternity. This being so, God could never act one way at one time and another way later on. Circumstances may differ and cases may differ, but in principle the will and ways of God are just the same today as they were in the days of the Acts.

God said to the Israelites, "Moses, because of your hardness of heart, allowed you to divorce your wives" (Matt. 19:8), but the Lord Jesus said, "What God has yoked together, let man not separate" (Matt. 19:6). Is there not a discrepancy here? No! "Moses, because of your hardness of heart, allowed you to divorce your wives, but from the beginning it has not been so" (Matt. 19:8). It is not that in the beginning it was permissible, and later it became forbidden, and still later became permissible again, as though God were a changeable God. No, the Lord said, "From the beginning it has not been so" showing that God's will had never altered. From the beginning right on until today it is just the same. Here is a most important principle. If we want to know the mind of God, we must look at His commands in Genesis and not look at His permissions later on, because every later permission has this explanation, "because of your hardness of heart." It is God's directive will we want to discover, not His permissive will. We want to see what God's purpose was from the beginning. We want to see things as they were when they proceeded in all their purity from the mind of God, not what they have become because of hardness of heart on the part of His people.

If we would understand the will of God concerning His Church, then we must not look to see how He led His people last year, or ten years ago, or a hundred years ago, but we must return to the beginning, to the "genesis" of the Church, to see what He said and did then. It is there we find the highest expression of His will. Acts is the "genesis" of the Church's history, and the Church in the time of Paul is the "genesis" of the Spirit's work. Conditions in the Church today are vastly different from what they were then, but these present conditions could never be our example, or our authoritative guide. We must return to the beginning. Only what God has set forth as our example in the beginning is the eternal will of God. It is the divine standard and our pattern for all time.

A word of explanation may be needed regarding the examples God has given us in His Word. Christianity is not only built upon precepts, but also upon examples. God has revealed His will, not only by giving orders, but by having certain things done in His Church, so that in the ages to come others might simply look at the pattern and know His will. God has not only directed His people by means of abstract principles and objective regulations, but by concrete examples and subjective experience. God does use precepts to teach His people, but one of His chief methods of instruction is through history. God tells us how others knew and did His will, so that we, by looking at their lives, may not only know His will, but see how to do it too. He worked in their lives, producing in them what He Himself desired, and He bids us look at them, so that we may know what He is after.

Shall we, then, say that because God has not commanded a certain thing we need not do it? If we have seen His dealings with men in days past, if we have seen how He led His people and built up His Church, can we still plead ignorance of His will? Is it necessary for a child to be told explicitly how to do everything? Must each item be separately mentioned of things permissible and not permissible? Are there not many things he can learn simply by watching his parents or his elder brothers and sisters? We learn more readily by what we see than by what we hear, and the impression upon us is deeper. That is why God has given us so much history in the Old Testament, and the Acts of the Apostles in the New. He knows we learn more easily by example than by precept. Examples have greater value than precepts, because precepts are abstract, while examples are precepts carried into effect. By looking at them, we not only know what God's precepts are, but we have a tangible demonstration of their outworking. If we try to eliminate examples from Christianity and leave only its precepts, then we have not much left. Precepts have their place, but examples have no less important a place, though obviously conformity to the divine pattern in outward things is mere formality if there is no correspondence in inner life.

In closing, may I stress the fact that this is not a book on missionary methods. Methods are not to be despised, but in God's service what matters most is the man, not his methods. Unless the man is right, right methods will be of no use to him or to his work. Carnal methods are suited to carnal men, and spiritual methods to spiritual men. For carnal men to employ spiritual methods will only result in confusion and failure. This book is intended for those who, having learned something of the cross, know the corruption of human nature, and seek to walk, not after the flesh, but after the Spirit. Its object is to help those who acknowledge the lordship of Christ in all things, and are seeking to serve Him in the way of His own appointing, not of their choosing. To put it in other words, it is written for those who are already in the good of Ephesian truths, so that they may know how to express their service along Corinthian lines. May none of my readers use this book as a basis for external adjustments in their work, without letting the cross deal drastically with their natural life.

In God's work everything depends upon the kind of worker sent out and the kind of convert produced. On the part of the convert, a real Holy Spirit new birth is essential, and a vital relationship with God. On the part of the worker, besides personal holiness and enduement for service, it is essential that he have an experimental knowledge of the meaning of committal to God and faith in His sovereign providence. Otherwise, no matter how scriptural the methods employed, the result will be emptiness and defeat.

To the Lord and to His people I commend this book, with the prayer that He may use it for His glory, as He sees fit.

Shanghai
January 1938
W. Nee

Chapter One

THE APOSTLES

God is a God of works. Our Lord said, "My Father is working until now." And He has a definite purpose toward the realization of which He directs all His works. He is the God "who works all things according to the counsel of His will." But God does not do everything directly by Himself. He works through His servants. Among the servants of God the apostles are the most important ones. Let us look into the Word of God to see what it has to teach on the matter of the apostles.

THE FIRST APOSTLE

In the fullness of time, God sent forth His Son into the world to do His work. He is known as the Christ of God, that is, "the Anointed One." The term "Son" relates to His Person; the name "Christ" relates to His office. He was the Son of God, but He was sent to be the Christ of God. "Christ" is the ministerial name of the Son of God. Our Lord did not come to the earth or to the cross on His own initiative; He was anointed and set apart for the work by God. He was not self-appointed, but sent. Frequently throughout the Gospel of John we find Him referring to God, not as "God," or "the Father," but as "Him who sent Me." He took the place of a sent one. If that is true in the case of the Son of God, how much more should it apply to His servants? If even the Son was not expected to take any initiative in God's work, is it likely that we are expected to do so? The first principle to note in the work of God is that all His workers are sent ones. If there is no divine commission, there can be no divine work.

Scripture has a special name for a sent one, that is, an apostle. The meaning of the Greek word is "the sent one."

The Lord Himself is the first Apostle because He is the first one specially sent of God; hence, the Word refers to Him as "the Apostle" (Heb. 3:1).

THE TWELVE

While our Lord fulfilled His apostolic ministry on earth, He was all the time aware that His life in the flesh was limited. Therefore, even as He pursued the work committed to Him by the Father, He was preparing a group of men to continue it after His departure. These men were also termed apostles. They were not volunteers; they were sent ones. We cannot overemphasize this fact that all divine work is by commission, not by choice.

From among whom did our Lord choose these apostles? They were chosen from among His disciples. All those sent out by the Lord were already disciples. Not all disciples are necessarily apostles, but all apostles are necessarily disciples; not all disciples are chosen for the work, but those who are chosen are always selected from among the disciples of the Lord. An apostle then must have two callings; in the first place he must be called to be a disciple, and in the second place he must be called to be an apostle. His first calling is from among the children of the world to be a follower of the Lord. His second calling is from among the followers of the Lord to be a sent one of the Lord.

Those apostles chosen by our Lord during His earthly ministry occupy a special place in Scripture, and they also occupy a special place in the purpose of God, because they were with the Son of God while He lived in the flesh. They were not just called apostles; they were called "the twelve apostles." They occupy a special place in the Word of God, and they occupy a special place in the plan of God. Our Lord told Peter that one day they should "sit on thrones judging the twelve tribes of Israel" (Luke 22:30). The Apostle has His throne, and the twelve apostles are going to have their thrones too. This is a privilege not granted to other apostles. When Judas lost his office and God led the remaining eleven to choose one to make up the number, we read that they cast lots and the lot fell upon Matthias, "and he was counted with the eleven apostles" (Acts 1:26). In the next chapter we find the Holy Spirit inspiring the writer of the Acts to say, "Peter, standing with the eleven" (Acts 2:14), which shows that the Holy Spirit recognized Matthias to be one of the twelve. Here we see that the number of these apostles was fixed; God did not want more than twelve, nor would He have less. In the book of Revelation we find that the ultimate position which they occupy is again a special one—"And the wall of the city had twelve foundations, and on them the twelve names of the twelve apostles of the Lamb" (Rev. 21:14). Even in the new heaven and the new earth the twelve enjoy a place of particular privilege, which is assigned to no other workers for God.

THE APOSTLES IN SCRIPTURE DAYS

The Lord as an apostle was unique, and the twelve, as apostles, were also unique; but neither the Apostle nor the twelve apostles could abide on earth forever. When our Lord departed, He left the twelve to continue His work. Now that the twelve have departed, who are here to carry it on?

The Lord has gone, but the Spirit has come. The Holy Spirit is come to bear all responsibility for the work of God on earth. The Son was working for the Father; the Spirit is working for the Son. The Son came to accomplish the will of the Father; the Spirit has come to accomplish the will of the Son. The Son came to glorify the Father; the Spirit has come to glorify the Son. The Father appointed Christ to be the Apostle; the Son while on earth appointed the twelve to be apostles. Now the Son has returned to the Father, and the Spirit is on earth appointing men to be apostles. The apostles appointed by the Holy Spirit cannot join the ranks of those appointed by the Son; nevertheless, they are apostles. The apostles we read of in Ephesians 4 are clearly not the original twelve, for *those* were appointed when the Lord was still on earth, while *these* date their appointment to apostleship after the ascension of the Lord—they were the gifts of the Lord Jesus to His Church *after* His glorification. The apostles *then* were the personal followers of the Lord Jesus, but the apostles *now* are ministers for the building up of the Body of Christ. We must differentiate clearly between the apostles who were witnesses to the resurrection of Christ (Acts 1:22, 26), and the apostles who are ministers for the edifying of the Body of Christ, for the Body of Christ was not in existence before the cross. There is no doubt that later on the twelve received the Ephesian commission, but the twelve, as the twelve, were quite distinct from the apostles mentioned in Ephesians. It is evident then that God has *other* apostles besides the original twelve.

Immediately after the outpouring of the Spirit we see the twelve apostles carrying on the work. Until Acts 12 they are seen as the chief workers; but with the opening of chapter thirteen we see the Holy Spirit beginning to manifest Himself as the Agent of Christ and the Lord of the Church. In that chapter we are told that in Antioch, when certain prophets and teachers were ministering to the Lord and fasting, the Holy Spirit said, "Set apart for Me now Barnabas and Saul for the work to which I have called them" (Acts 13:2). Now is the time that the Spirit begins to send men forth. At this point two new workers were commissioned by the Holy Spirit.

After these two were sent out by the Spirit, how were they designated? When Barnabas and Paul were working in Iconium, "the multitude of the city was divided, and some were with the Jews and some with the apostles" (Acts 14:4). The two sent forth in the previous chapter are in this chapter referred to as apostles, and in the same chapter (v. 14), the designation "the apostles" is used in apposition to "Barnabas and Paul," which proves conclusively that the two men commissioned by the Holy Spirit were also apostles. They were not among the twelve; nevertheless, they were apostles.

Who then are apostles? Apostles are God's workmen, sent out by the Holy Spirit to do the work to which He has called them. The responsibility of the work is in their hands. Broadly speaking, all believers are responsible for the work of God, but apostles are a group of people specially set apart for the work. In a particular sense the responsibility of the work is upon them.

Now we see the teaching of the Scriptures as touching apostles. God appointed His Son to be the Apostle; Christ appointed His disciples to be the twelve apostles; and the

Holy Spirit appointed a group of men (apart from the twelve) to be the Body-building apostles. The first Apostle is unique; there is only one. The twelve apostles are also in a class by themselves; there are only twelve. But there is another order of apostles, chosen by the Holy Spirit, and as long as the building up of the Church goes on and the Holy Spirit's presence on earth continues, the choosing and sending forth of this order of apostles will continue too.

In the Word of God we find numerous other apostles besides Barnabas and Paul. There are many belonging to the new order chosen and sent forth by the Spirit of God. In 1 Corinthians 4:9 we read, "God has set forth us the apostles last." To whom do the words "us the apostles" refer? The pronoun "us" implies that there was at least one other apostle besides the writer. If we study the context, we note that Apollos was with Paul when he wrote (v. 6), and Sosthenes was a joint writer with Paul of the Epistle. So it seems clear that the "us" here refers either to Apollos or to Sosthenes, or to both. It follows then that either or both of these two must have been apostles.

Romans 16:7: "Greet Andronicus and Junia, my kinsmen and my fellow prisoners, who are of note among the apostles." The clause "who are of note among the apostles" does not mean that they were regarded as notable by the apostles, but rather that among the apostles they were notable ones. Here we have not only another two apostles, but another two notable apostles.

First Thessalonians 2:6: "We could have stood on our authority as apostles of Christ." The "we" here refers clearly to the writers of the Thessalonian letter, that is, Paul, Silvanus, and Timothy (1:1), which indicates that Paul's two young fellow workers were also apostles.

First Corinthians 15:5-7: "He appeared to Cephas, then to the twelve; then He appeared to over five hundred brothers at one time,...then He appeared to James, then to all the apostles." Besides the twelve apostles there was a group known as "all the apostles." It is obvious, then, that apart from the twelve, there were other apostles.

Paul never claimed that he was the last apostle and that

after him there were no others. Let us read carefully what he said: "Last of all He appeared to me also...for I am the least of the apostles, who am not fit to be called an apostle" (1 Cor. 15:8-9). Notice how Paul used the words "last" and "least." He did not say that he was the last apostle; he only said he was the least apostle. If he were the last, there could be no more after him, but he was only the least.

In the book of Revelation it is said of the Ephesian church: "You have tried those who call themselves apostles and are not, and have found them to be false" (2:2). It seems clear from this verse that the early churches expected to have other apostles apart from the original twelve, because, when the book of Revelation was written, John was the only survivor of the twelve, and by that time even Paul had already been martyred. If there were to be only twelve apostles, and John was the only one left, then no one would have been foolish enough to pose as an apostle, and no one foolish enough to be deceived, and where would have been the need to try them? If John were the only apostle, then testing would be simple indeed! Anyone who was not John was not an apostle!

THE MEANING OF APOSTLESHIP

Since the meaning of the word "apostle" is "the sent one," the meaning of apostleship is quite plain, that is, the office of the sent one. Apostles are not primarily men of special gifts; they are men of special commission. Everyone who is sent of God is an apostle. Many called of God are not as gifted as Paul, but if they have received a commission from God, they are just as truly apostles as he was. The apostles were gifted men, but their apostleship was not based upon their gifts; it was based upon their commission. Of course, God will not send anyone who is unequipped, but equipment does not constitute apostleship. If God cared to send out a man totally unequipped, that man would be as much an apostle as a fully equipped one, since apostleship is not based on human qualification but on divine commission. It is futile for anyone to assume the office of an apostle simply because he thinks he has the needed gifts or ability. It takes more than mere gift and ability to constitute men apostles; it takes nothing less than God Himself, God's will, and God's call. No man can attain to apostleship through natural or other qualifications; God must make him an apostle if he is ever to be one. Whether or not a man is going to be of any spiritual worth, and his work serve any spiritual end, depends upon the sending of God. "A man sent of God" should be the main characteristic of our entering upon His service, and of all our subsequent movements.

Let us turn to the Scriptures. In Luke 11:49 we read, "I will send to them prophets and apostles, and some of them they will kill and persecute." From Genesis to Malachi we do not come across anyone who was explicitly called an apostle; yet the men here referred to as apostles lived between the time of Abel and Zachariah (v. 51). Therefore, it is clear that even in Old Testament times God had His apostles.

Our Lord said, "A slave is not greater than his master, nor the apostle [Greek] greater than the one who sends him" (John 13:16). Here we have a definition of the term "apostle." It implies being sent out—that is all; and that is everything. However good human intention may be, it can never take the place of divine commission. Today those who have been sent out by the Lord to preach the gospel and to establish churches call themselves missionaries, not apostles; but the word "missionary" means the very same thing as "apostle," that is, "the sent one." It is the Latin form of the Greek equivalent, *apostolos*. Since the meaning of the two words is exactly the same, I fail to see the reason why the *true* sent ones of today prefer to call themselves missionaries rather than apostles.

APOSTLES AND THE MINISTRY

"But to each one of us grace was given according to the measure of the gift of Christ. Therefore the Scripture says, 'Having ascended to the height, He led captive those taken captive and gave gifts to men.' (Now this, 'He ascended,' what is it except that He also descended into the lower parts of the earth? He who descended, He is also the One who ascended far above all the heavens that He might fill all things.) And He Himself gave some[1] as apostles and some as prophets and some as evangelists and some as shepherds and teachers, for the perfecting of the saints unto the work of the ministry, unto the building up of the Body of Christ, until we all arrive at the oneness of the faith and of the full knowledge of the Son of God, at a full-grown man, at the measure of the stature of the fullness of Christ" (Eph. 4:7-13).

There are many ministries connected with the service of God, but He has chosen a number of men for a special ministry—the ministry of the Word for the building up of the Body of Christ. Since that ministry is different from others, we refer to it as "the ministry." This ministry is entrusted to a group of people of whom the apostles are chief. It is neither a one-man ministry, nor an "all-men" ministry, but a ministry based upon the gifts of the Holy Spirit and an experimental knowledge of the Lord.

Apostles, prophets, evangelists, and shepherds and teachers are our Lord's gifts to His Church to serve in the ministry. Strictly speaking, shepherds and teachers are one gift, not two, because teaching and shepherding are closely related. In enumerating the gifts, apostles, prophets, and evangelists are all mentioned separately, while shepherds and teachers are linked together. Furthermore, the first three are each prefixed by the word "some," whereas the word "some" is attached to shepherds and teachers unitedly, thus—"some as apostles," "some as prophets," "some as evangelists," and "some as shepherds and teachers," not "some as shepherds and some as teachers." The fact that the word "some" is used only four times in this list indicates that there are only four classes of persons in question. Shepherds and teachers are two in one.

Shepherding and teaching may be regarded as one ministry, because those who teach must also shepherd, and those who shepherd must also teach. The two kinds of work are interrelated. Furthermore, the word "shepherd" as applied to any person is found nowhere else in the New Testament, but the word "teacher" is used on four other occasions. In the New Testament we find reference elsewhere to an apostle (for

---

[1] See also Panin and Interlinear.

example, Paul), and a prophet (for example, Agabus), and an evangelist (for example, Philip), and a teacher (for example, Manaen), but nowhere in God's Word do we find anyone referred to as a shepherd. This confirms the fact that shepherds and teachers are one class of men.

Teachers are men who have received the gift of teaching. This is not a miraculous gift, but a gift of grace, which accounts for the fact of its being omitted from the list of miraculous gifts in 1 Corinthians 12:8-10, and included in the list of the gifts of grace in Romans 12. It is a gift of grace which enables its possessors to understand the teachings of God's Word, and to discern His purposes, and thus equips them to instruct His people in doctrinal matters. In the church in Antioch there were several persons thus equipped, Paul among the number. It is by the operation of God that such men are "placed...in the church," and their position is next to that of the prophets. A teacher is an individual who has received the gift of teaching from God, and has been given by the Lord to His Church for its upbuilding. The work of a teacher is to interpret to others the truths which have been revealed to him, to lead God's people to an understanding of the Word, and to encourage them to seek and receive for themselves divine revelation through the Scriptures. Their sphere of work is mainly among the children of God, though at times they also teach the unsaved (1 Tim. 4:11; 6:2; 2 Tim. 2:2; Acts 4:2-18; 5:21, 25, 28, 42). Their work is more one of interpretation than of revelation, whereas the work of the prophets is more one of revelation than of interpretation. They seek to lead believers to an understanding of divine truth, and they seek to lead unbelievers to an understanding of the gospel.

Evangelists are also our Lord's gift to His Church, but exactly what their personal gifts are we do not know. The Word of God does not speak of any evangelistic gift, but it does refer to Philip as being an evangelist (Acts 21:8), and Paul on one occasion encouraged Timothy to do the work of an evangelist and fill up the measure of his ministry (2 Tim. 4:5). Apart from these three occasions, the noun "evangelist" is not found in Scripture, though we frequently meet the verb which is derived from the same root.

In the Word of God the place of prophets is more clearly defined than that of teachers and evangelists. Prophecy is mentioned among the gifts of grace (Rom. 12:6), and among the miraculous gifts we find it again (1 Cor. 12:10). God has set prophets in the Church universal (1 Cor. 12:28), but He has also given prophets for the ministry (Eph. 4:11). There is both the gift of prophecy and the office of a prophet. Prophecy is both a gift of miracle and a gift of grace. The prophet is both a man set by God in His Church to occupy the prophetic office, and a man given by the Lord to His Church for the ministry.

Of the four classes of gifted men bestowed by the Lord upon His Church for its upbuilding, the apostles were quite different from the other three. The special position occupied by apostles is obvious to any reader of the New Testament. They were specially commissioned of God to found churches through the preaching of the gospel, to bring revelation from God to His people, to give decisions in matters pertaining to doctrine and government, and to edify the saints and distribute the gifts. Both spiritually and geographically their sphere is vast. That their position was superior to that of prophets and teachers is clear from the Word: "God has placed some in the church: first apostles" (1 Cor. 12:28).

Apostles belong to the ministry, but they are quite different from the prophets, evangelists, and teachers, because, unlike these three, it is not their gifts that determine their office; that is, they are not constituted apostles by receiving an apostolic gift.

It is important to note that apostleship is an office, not a gift. An office is what one receives as the result of a commission; a gift is what one receives on the basis of grace. "I was appointed...an apostle" (1 Tim. 2:7). "I was appointed...an apostle" (2 Tim. 1:11). We see here that apostles are commissioned. Being an apostle is not subject to receiving an apostolic gift, but subject to receiving an apostolic commission. An apostle has a special call and a special commission. It is in this that he differs from the other three ministers, though he may have received the prophetic gift and thus be a prophet as well as an apostle. His personal gift constitutes him a prophet, but it is commission, not gift, that constitutes him an apostle. The other ministers belong to the ministry by virtue of their gifts; an apostle belongs to the ministry by virtue of his being sent. *Their* qualification is the possession of gifts; *his* is the possession of gifts plus a special call and commission.

An apostle may be a prophet or a teacher. Should he exercise his gift of prophecy or teaching in the local church, he does so in the capacity of a prophet or a teacher, but when he exercises his gifts in different places, he does so in the capacity of an apostle. The implication of apostleship is being sent of God to exercise gifts of ministry in different places. It is immaterial to his office what personal gift an apostle has, but it is essential to his office that he be sent of God. An apostle can exercise his spiritual gifts in any place, but he cannot exercise his apostolic gifts, because an apostle is such by office, not by gift.

Nevertheless, apostles have personal gifts for their ministry. "Now there were in Antioch, in the local church, *prophets and teachers:* Barnabas and Simeon, who was called Niger, and Lucius the Cyrenian, and Manaen, the foster brother of Herod the tetrarch, and Saul. And as they were ministering to the Lord and fasting, the Holy Spirit said, Set apart for Me now Barnabas and Saul for the work to which I have called them" (Acts 13:1-2). These five men had the gifts of prophecy and teaching, a miraculous gift and a gift of grace. From that company of five *two* were sent by the Spirit to other parts, and *three* were left in Antioch. As we have already seen, the two sent out were thereafter *called apostles.* They received no apostolic gift, but they did receive an apostolic commission. It was their gifts that qualified them to be prophets and teachers, but it was their commission that qualified them to be apostles. The three who remained in Antioch *were still prophets and teachers,* not apostles, simply because they had not been sent out by the Spirit. The two became apostles, not because they had received any gift in addition to the gift of prophecy and teaching, but because they received an additional office as a result of their commission. The gifts of all five were just the same, but the two received a divine commission in addition to their gifts, and that qualified them for apostolic ministry.

Then why does the Word of God say, "He Himself gave some as apostles"? It is not a question here of apostleship being a gift given to an apostle, but a gift given to the Church; it is not a spiritual gift given to a man, but a gifted man given to the Church. Ephesians 4:11 does not say that the Lord gave an apostolic gift to any person, but that He gave men as apostles to His Church. Men have received gifts of the Spirit which have qualified them to become prophets and teachers, but no man has ever received a spiritual gift which has qualified him to be an apostle. Apostles are a class of people the Church has received as our Lord's gift for its upbuilding.

The gifts referred to in this passage are not the gifts given to men personally, but the gifts given by the Lord to His Church, and the gifts mentioned here are gifted workers whom the Lord of the Church bestows upon His Church for its edification. The Head gives to the Church which is His Body certain *men* to serve the Body and build it up. *We must distinguish between those gifts given by the Spirit to individuals and those given by the Lord to His Church.* The former are given to believers personally; the latter are given to believers corporately. The former are things, and the latter are persons. The gifts given by the Spirit to individuals are their equipment to serve the Lord in prophesy, teaching, speaking in tongues, and healing the sick; the gifts given by the Lord to His Church as a Body are the persons who possess the gifts of the Spirit.

"For to one through the Spirit a word of wisdom is given, and to another a word of knowledge, according to the same Spirit; to a different one faith in the same Spirit, and to another gifts of healing in the one Spirit, and to another operations of works of power, and to another prophecy, and to another discerning of spirits; to a different one various kinds of tongues, and to another interpretation of tongues" (1 Cor. 12:8-10). This passage provides us with a list of all the gifts which the Holy Spirit gave to men, but it includes no apostolic gift. "And God has placed some in the church: first apostles, second prophets, third teachers; then works of power, then gifts of healing, helps, administrations, various kinds of tongues" (1 Cor. 12:28). The first passage enumerates the gifts given to individuals; the second enumerates the gifts given to the Church. In the former there is no mention of any apostolic gift; in the latter we find that apostles head the list of God's gifts to the Church. It is not that God has given His Church the gift of apostleship, but that He has given it *men* who are apostles; and He has not given the gifts of prophecy and teaching to His Church, but He has given it some men as prophets and some as teachers. God has set different kinds of workers in His Church for its edification, one of which is apostles. They do not represent a certain kind of gift; they represent a certain class of persons.

The difference between the apostles, and the prophets and teachers, is that the latter two represent both gifts given by the Spirit to individuals and at the same time gifts given by the Lord to His Church, whereas apostles are men given by the Lord to His Church, but they do not represent any special, personal gift of the Spirit.

"And God has placed some in the church: first apostles, second prophets, third teachers" (1 Cor. 12:28). What church is this? It comprises all the children of God; therefore, it is the Church universal. In this Church God has set "first apostles, second prophets, third teachers." In 1 Corinthians 14:23 we read that "the whole church comes together." What church is this? Obviously the local church, for the Church universal cannot gather together in one locality. It is in this local church that the brethren exercised their spiritual gifts. One would have a psalm, another a teaching, another a revelation, another a tongue, and another an interpretation (14:26), but more important than all these was the gift of prophecy (14:1). In chapter twelve, apostles took precedence over the other ministers, but in chapter fourteen, prophets take the precedence. In the Church universal, apostles are first, but in the local church, prophets are first. How does it come about that prophets take first place in the local church, since in the universal Church they only occupy the second place? Because in the Church universal the question is not of personal gifts of the Spirit, but of God's gift of *ministers* to the Church, and of these, apostles rank first; but in the local church the question is one of *personal gifts* of the Spirit, and of these, prophecy is chief, because *it is most important.* Let us remember that apostleship is not a personal gift.

THE SPHERE OF THEIR WORK

The sphere of an apostle's work is quite different from that of the other three special ministers. That prophets and teachers exercise their gifts in the local church is seen from the statement: "Now there were in Antioch, in the local church, prophets and teachers." You can find prophets and teachers in the local church, but not apostles, because they have been called to minister in different places, while the ministry of prophets and teachers is confined to one locality (1 Cor. 14:26, 29).

As to evangelists, we do not know their special sphere, as very little is said of them in God's Word, but the story of Philip, the evangelist, throws some light on this class of ministers. Philip left his own locality and preached in Samaria, but while he did good work there, the Spirit did not fall upon any of his converts. It was not till the apostles came from Jerusalem and laid hands on them that the Spirit was poured out. This *seems to indicate* that the local preaching of the gospel is the work of an evangelist, but the universal preaching of the gospel is the work of an apostle. This does not imply that the labors of an evangelist are necessarily confined to one place, but it does mean that that is their usual sphere. In the same way the prophet Agabus prophesied in another place, but his special sphere of work was his own locality.

THE EVIDENCE OF APOSTLESHIP

Is there any evidence that one is really commissioned of God to be an apostle? In 1 Corinthians 9:1-2, Paul is dealing with our question in writing to the Corinthian saints, and it is obvious from his argument that apostleship has its credentials. "For you in the Lord are the seal of my apostleship," he writes, as if to say, "If God had not sent me to Corinth, then you would not be saved today, and there would be no church in your city." If God has called a man to be an apostle, it will be manifest in the fruit of his labors. Wherever you have the commission of God, there you have the authority of God; wherever you have the authority of God, there you have the power of God; and wherever you have the power of God, there you have spiritual fruits. The fruit of our labors proves the validity of our commission. And yet it must be noted that Paul's thought is not that apostleship implies numerous converts, but that it represents spiritual values to the Lord, for He could never send anyone forth for a lesser purpose. The Lord is out for spiritual values, and the object of apostleship is to secure them. In this case the Corinthians represent these values. But did not Paul say here, "Have I not seen Jesus our Lord?" Then is it only those who have seen the Lord Jesus in His resurrection manifestations who are qualified to become apostles? Let us follow carefully the trend of Paul's argument. In verse 1 he asks four questions: (1) "Am I not free?" (2) "Am I not an apostle?" (3) "Have I not seen Jesus our Lord?" (4) "Are you not my work in the Lord?" An affirmative answer to all four questions was taken for granted, for Paul's case demanded such an answer. Notice that in pursuing his argument in the second verse, Paul drops two of his questions and follows out the other two. He drops the first and third, and takes up the second and fourth, linking them together. For the purpose of his reasoning he sets aside, "Am I not free?" and, "Have I not seen Jesus our Lord?" and replies to the question, "Am I not an apostle?" and, "Are you not my work in the Lord?" Paul was clearly seeking to demonstrate the genuineness of his commission from the blessing that attended his labors, not from his being free or from his having seen the Lord.

Of the four questions asked by Paul, three relate to his person and one to his work. These three are on the same plane, and are quite independent of one another. Paul was not arguing that because he was free and because he was an apostle, therefore he had seen the Lord. Nor was he reasoning that because he was an apostle and because he had seen the Lord, therefore he was free. Neither was he seeking to demonstrate that because he was free and had seen the Lord, therefore he was an apostle. The facts are he *was* free, he *was* an apostle, and he *had* seen the Lord. These facts had *no* essential connection one with the other, and it is absurd to connect them. It would be as reasonable to argue that Paul's apostleship was based upon his being free, as that it was based upon his seeing the Lord. If he was not seeking to prove his apostleship from the fact of his freedom, neither was he seeking to prove it from his having seen the Lord. Apostleship is not based on having seen the Lord in His resurrection manifestations.

Then what is the meaning of 1 Corinthians 15:5-9? "He appeared to Cephas, then to the twelve; then He appeared to over five hundred brothers at one time,...then He appeared to James, then to all the apostles; and last of all He appeared to me also." The object of this passage is not to produce evidence of apostleship, but evidence of the resurrection of the Lord. Paul is recording the different persons to whom the Lord appeared; he is not teaching what *effect* was produced upon these persons by His appearing. Cephas and James saw the Lord, but they were Cephas and James after they saw the Lord, just as they were Cephas and James before; they did not become Cephas and James by seeing Him. The same applies to the twelve apostles and the five hundred brethren. Seeing the Lord did not constitute them apostles. They were twelve apostles before they saw the Lord, and they were twelve apostles after they saw the Lord. The same argument applies in Paul's case. The facts were that he had seen the Lord, and he was the least of the apostles; but it was not seeing the Lord that constituted him the least of the apostles. The five hundred brethren were not apostles before they saw the Lord, nor were they after. Seeing the Lord in His resurrection manifestations did not constitute them apostles. They were simply brethren before, and they were simply brethren after. The Word of God nowhere teaches that seeing the Lord is the qualification for apostleship.

But apostleship has its credentials. In 2 Corinthians

12:11-12, Paul writes, "In nothing am I inferior to the super-apostles.... Indeed the signs of an apostle were wrought among you in all endurance by signs and wonders and works of power." There was abundant evidence of the genuineness of Paul's apostolic commission; and the signs of an apostle will never be lacking where there is truly an apostolic call. From the above passage we infer that the evidence of apostleship lies in a twofold power—spiritual and miraculous. Endurance is the greatest proof of spiritual power, and it is one of the signs of an apostle. It is the ability to endure steadfastly under continuous pressure that tests the reality of an apostolic call. A true apostle needs to be "empowered with all power, according to the might of His glory, unto all endurance and long-suffering with joy" (Col. 1:11). Yes, it takes nothing short of "all power, according to the might of His glory" to produce "all endurance and long-suffering with joy." But the reality of Paul's apostleship was not only attested by his patient endurance under intense and prolonged pressure; it was evidenced also by the miraculous power he possessed. Miraculous power to change situations in the physical world is a necessary manifestation of our knowledge of God in the spiritual realm, and this applies not to heathen lands only, but to every land. To profess to be sent ones of the omnipotent God, and yet stand helpless before situations that challenge His power, is a sad contradiction. Not all who can work wonders are apostles, for the gifts of healing and of miracle-working are given to members of the Body (1 Cor. 12:28) who have no special commission, but miraculous as well as spiritual power is part of the equipment of all who have a true apostolic commission.

WOMEN APOSTLES

Have women any place among the ranks of the apostles? Scripture indicates that they have. There were no women among the twelve sent forth by the Lord, but a woman is mentioned among the number of the apostles who were sent forth by the Spirit after the Lord's ascension. Romans 16:7 speaks of two notable apostles, Andronicus and Junia, and good authorities agree that "Junia" is a woman's name. So here we have a sister as an apostle and a notable apostle at that.

Chapter Two

THE SEPARATION AND MOVEMENTS OF THE APOSTLES

ANTIOCH—THE MODEL CHURCH

The church in Antioch is the model church shown us in God's Word, because it was the first to come into being after the founding of the churches connected with the Jews and the Gentiles. In Acts 2 we see the church in connection with the Jews established in Jerusalem, and in chapter ten we see the church in connection with the Gentiles established in the house of Cornelius. It was just after the establishment of these churches that the church in Antioch was founded. In its transition stage the church in Jerusalem was not altogether free from Judaism, but the church in Antioch from the very outset stood on absolutely clear Church ground. It is of no little significance that "the disciples were first called Christians in Antioch" (Acts 11:26). It was there that the peculiar characteristics of the Christian and the Christian Church were first clearly manifested, for which reason it may be regarded as the pattern church for this dispensation. Its prophets and teachers were model prophets and teachers, and the apostles it sent forth were model apostles. Not only are the men sent forth an example to us, but the manner of their sending forth is our example too. Since the first recorded sending out of apostles by the Holy Spirit was from Antioch, we shall do well to look carefully into its details.

Since the completion of the New Testament the Holy Spirit has called many of God's children to serve Him throughout the world, but, strictly speaking, none of these can be regarded as our examples. We must always look at the first act of the Holy Spirit in any given direction to discover His pattern for us in that particular direction. Therefore, in order to see what example the Church must follow today in the sending forth of apostles, let us examine carefully the first recorded sending forth of workers from the first church established on absolutely clear Church ground.

THE HOLY SPIRIT'S CALL

In the first two verses of Acts 13 we read, "Now there were in Antioch, in the local church, prophets and teachers: Barnabas and Simeon, who was called Niger, and Lucius the Cyrenian, and Manaen, the foster brother of Herod the tetrarch, and Saul. And as they were ministering to the Lord and fasting, the Holy Spirit said, Set apart for Me now Barnabas and Saul for the work to which I have called them." Let us note a few facts here. There was a local church in Antioch, there were certain prophets and teachers who were ministers in that church, and it was from among those that the Holy Spirit separated two for another sphere of service. Barnabas and Saul were two ministers of the Lord already engaged in the ministry when the call of the Spirit came. The Holy Spirit only sends to other parts such as are already equipped for the work and are bearing responsibility where they are, not those who are burying their talents and neglecting local needs while they dream of some future day when the call will come to special service. Barnabas and Saul were bearing the burden of the local situation when the Spirit put the burden of other parts upon them. Their hands were full of local work when He thrust them out to work further afield. Let us note first that the Holy Spirit chooses apostles from among the prophets and teachers.

"And as they were ministering to the Lord and fasting, the Holy Spirit said, Set apart for Me now Barnabas and Saul for the work to which *I have called them.*" These prophets and teachers ministered so wholeheartedly to the Lord that when occasion demanded they even ignored the legitimate claims of their physical being and fasted. What filled the thoughts of those prophets and teachers at Antioch was ministry to the Lord, not work for Him. Their devotion was to the Lord Himself, not to His service. No one can truly work for the Lord who has not first learned to minister to

SEPARATION AND MOVEMENTS OF THE APOSTLES   21

Him. It was while Barnabas and Saul ministered to the Lord that the voice of the Spirit was heard calling them to special service.

It was to the divine call they responded, not to the call of human need. They had heard no reports of man-eaters or head-hunting savages; their compassions had not been stirred by doleful tales of child-marriage or foot-binding or opium-smoking. They had heard no voice but the voice of the Spirit; they had seen no claims but the claims of Christ. No appeal had been made to their natural heroism or love of adventure. They knew only one appeal—the appeal of their Lord. It was the lordship of Christ that claimed their service, and it was on His authority alone that they went forth. Their call was a spiritual call. No natural factor entered into it. It was the Holy Spirit who said, "Set apart for Me now Barnabas and Saul for the work to which I have called them." All spiritual work must begin with the Spirit's call. All divine work must be divinely initiated. The plan conceived for the work may be splendid, the reason adequate, the need urgent, and the man chosen to carry it out may be eminently suitable; but if the Holy Spirit has not said, "Set apart that man for the work to which I have called him," he can never be an apostle. He may be a prophet or a teacher, but he is no apostle. Of old all true apostles were separated by the Holy Spirit for the work to which He called them, and today all true apostles must just as surely be set apart for the work by Him. God desires the service of His children, but He makes conscripts; He wants no volunteers. The work is His, and He is its only legitimate Originator. Human intention, however good, can never take the place of divine initiation. Earnest desires for the salvation of sinners or for the edification of saints will never qualify a man for God's work. One qualification, and only one, is necessary—God must send him.

It was the Holy Spirit who said, "Set apart for Me now Barnabas and Saul for the work to which I have called them." Only the divine call can qualify for the apostolic office. In earthly governments there can be no service without commission, and the same holds true in the government of God. The tragedy in Christian work today is that so many of the workers have simply gone out; they have not been sent. It is divine commission that constitutes the call to divine work. Personal desire, friendly persuasions, the advice of one's elders, and the urge of opportunity—all these are factors on the natural plane, and they can never take the place of a spiritual call. That is something which must be registered in the human spirit by the Spirit of God.

When Barnabas and Saul were sent forth, the Spirit first called them, then the brethren confirmed the call. The brethren may say you have a call, and circumstances may seem to indicate it, but the question is whether or not *you* yourself have heard the call. If *you* are to go forth, then *you* are the one who must first hear the voice of the Spirit. We dare not disregard the opinion of the brethren, but their opinion is no substitute for a personal call from God. Even if they are confident that we have a call, and in that same confidence a company of God's people gladly sends us forth to the work, unless we ourselves know a direct speaking of God into our hearts, on the basis of the new covenant, then we go forth as the messengers of men, not as the apostles of God.

If God desires the service of any child of His, He Himself will call him to it, and He Himself will send him forth. The first requirement in divine work is a divine call. Everything hinges on this. A divine call gives God His rightful place, for it recognizes Him as the Originator of the work. Where there is no call from God, the work undertaken is not of divine origin, and it has no spiritual value. Divine work must be divinely initiated. A worker may be called directly by the Spirit, or indirectly through the reading of the Word, through preaching, or through circumstances; but whatever means God may use to make His will known to man, *His* voice must be the one heard through every other voice; *He* must be the one who speaks, no matter through what instrument the call may come. We must never be independent of the other members of the Body, but we must never forget that we receive all our directions from the Head; so we must be careful to preserve our spiritual independence, even while we cultivate a spirit of mutual dependence among the members. It is wrong to reject the opinion of fellow workers under the pretext of doing the will of God, but it is also wrong to accept their opinions as a substitute for the direct instructions of the Spirit of God.

SEPARATION OF WORKERS

Yes, it was the Holy Spirit who called Barnabas and Saul, but He said to the other prophets and teachers as well as to them, "Set apart for Me now Barnabas and Saul for the work to which I have called them." The Holy Spirit spoke directly to the apostles, but He also spoke indirectly through the prophets and teachers. What was said privately to the two was confirmed publicly through the other three. All apostles must have a personal revelation of God's will, but to make that alone the basis of their going forth is not sufficient. On the one hand, the opinion of others, however spiritual and however experienced, can never be a substitute for a direct call from God. On the other hand, a personal call, however definite, requires the confirmation of the representative members of the Body of Christ in the locality from which the workers go out.

Let us observe that the Holy Spirit did not say to the *church* in Antioch, "Set apart for Me now Barnabas and Saul." It was to the prophets and teachers He spoke. For God to make His will known to the entire assembly would scarcely have been practicable. Some of its members were spiritually mature, but others were only babes in Christ. Some were wholeheartedly devoted to the Lord, but it is highly improbable that all the members sought the Lord with such singleness of purpose that they could clearly differentiate between His will and their own ideas. God therefore spoke to a representative company in the church, to men of spiritual experience who were utterly devoted to His interest.

And here was the result: "When they had fasted and prayed and laid their hands on them, they sent them away" (Acts 13:3). The setting apart of the apostles by the prophets and teachers followed the call which came to them from the Spirit. The call was personal, the separation was corporate; and the one was not complete without the other. A direct call from God, and a confirmation of that call in the setting apart of the called ones by the prophets and teachers, is God's provision against free lances in His service.

The calling of an apostle is the Holy Spirit speaking directly to the one called. The separating of an apostle is the Holy Spirit speaking indirectly through the fellow workers of the called one. It is the Holy Spirit who takes the initiative both in the calling and separation of workers. Therefore, if the representative brethren of any assembly set men apart for the service of the Lord, they must ask themselves, Are we doing this on our own initiative, or as representing the Spirit of God? If they move without absolute assurance that they are acting on behalf of the Holy Spirit, then the separation of the worker has no spiritual value. They must be able to say of every worker they send forth, He was sent out by the Holy Spirit, not by man. No separation of workers should be done hastily or lightly. It was for this reason that fasting and prayer preceded the sending forth of Barnabas and Saul.

When Barnabas and Saul were separated for the work, there was prayer and fasting and the laying on of hands. The prayer and fasting was not merely in view of the immediate need of clear discernment regarding the will of God, but in view also of the coming need when the apostles would actually go forth. And the laying on of hands was not by way of ordination, for Barnabas and Saul were already ordained by the Holy Spirit. Here, as in the Old Testament, it was an expression of the perfect oneness of the two parties represented. It was as though the three sending forth the two said to them, "When you two members of the Body of Christ go forth, all the other members go with you. Your going is our going, and your work is our work." The laying on of hands was a testimony to the oneness of the Body of Christ. It meant that those who remained behind were one with those who went forth, and in full sympathy with them; and that, as they went, those at the base pledged themselves to follow them continually with prayerful interest and loving sympathy.

As regards all sent ones, they must pay attention to these two aspects in their separation for the service of God. On the one hand, there must be a direct call from God and a personal recognition of that call. On the other hand, there must be a confirmation of that call by the representative members of the Body of Christ. And as regards all who are responsible for the sending forth of others, they must on the one hand be in a position to receive the revelation of the Spirit and to discern the mind of the Lord; on the other hand, they must be able to enter sympathetically into the experience of those whom they, as the representative members of the Body of Christ, send forth in the name of the Lord. The principle that governed the sending forth of the first apostles still governs the sending forth of all apostles who are truly appointed by the Spirit to the work of God.

THE EXPRESSION OF THE BODY

On what ground did these prophets and teachers set certain men apart as apostles, and whom did these prophets and teachers represent? Why did they, and not the entire church, separate those workers? What is the significance of such separation, and what is the qualification required on the part of those who assume responsibility in the matter?

The first thing we must realize is that God has incorporated all His children into one Body. He recognizes no division of His people into various "churches" and missions. He has designed that all who are His shall live a corporate life, the life of a body among whose many members there is mutual consideration, mutual love, and mutual understanding. And He has purposed that not only the life, but also the ministry of His children, should be on the principle of the body, that it should be a matter of mutual helpfulness, mutual edification, and mutual service—the activity of the many members of one body. There are two aspects of the Body of Christ—life and ministry. The first half of Ephesians 4 speaks of the Body in relation to its ministry; the second half speaks of the Body in relation to its life. "Out from whom all the Body, being joined together and being knit together through every joint of the rich supply and through the operation in the measure of each one part, causes the growth of the Body unto the building up of itself in love" (v. 16). Here it is work that is under consideration. But in verse 25 the question is clearly one of life: "Therefore having put off the lie, speak truth each one with his neighbor, for we are members one of another." In Romans 12 we see how the members should care one for another, so that the thought there again is the manifestation of the one life. But in 1 Corinthians 12 we see how the members should serve one another, so the thought in that passage is the manifestation of the one ministry.

When we speak of the one Body, we emphasize the oneness of the life of all God's children. When we speak of its many members, we emphasize the diversity of functions in that unity. The characteristic of the former is life; the characteristic of the latter is work. In a physical body the members differ one from another; yet they function as one, because they share one life and have the upbuilding of the whole body as their one aim.

Because the Body of Christ has these two different aspects—life and ministry—it consequently has two different outward manifestations. The church in a locality is used to express the life of the Body, and the gifts in the Church are used to express the ministry of its members. In other words, each local church should stand on the ground of the Body, regarding itself as an expression of the oneness of the life of the Body, and it should on no account admit of division, since it exists as the manifestation of an indivisible life. The various ministers of the Church should likewise stand on the ground of the Body, regarding themselves as an expression of the oneness of its varied ministries. Perfect fellowship and cooperation should characterize all their activity, for though their functions are diverse, their ministry is really one. No local church should divide into different sects, or affiliate with other churches under a denomination, thus departing from the ground of the Body; and no group of ministers should unite to form a separate unit, standing on other than Body ground. All their work should be performed as members of the Body, and not as members of an organization existing in distinction from it. A worker may employ his gifts in the capacity of an officer of an organization, but in so doing he departs from the ground of the Body.

A cursory reading of Ephesians 4:11-12 might lead us to conclude that apostles, prophets, evangelists, shepherds and teachers functioned outside the Body, because they were given by the Lord to His Church for her upbuilding (v. 12). But verse 16 makes it clear that they do not stand outside the Body to build it up; they seek to build it up from within. They themselves are part of the Body, and it is only as they take their rightful place in it, as ministering members, that the whole Body is edified.

That churches are the local expression of the Body of Christ is an established fact, so we need not go into that here; but some explanation is called for regarding the gifted ministers whom God has set in the Church as the expression of the ministry of the Body. In 1 Corinthians 12 Paul is clearly dealing with the question of Christian service. He likens the workers to different members of a body, and shows that each member has its specific use, and all serve the body as belonging to it, not as distinct from it. In verse 27 he writes, "Now you are the body of Christ, and members individually"; and in the following verse he says, "And God has placed some in the church: first apostles, second prophets, third teachers; then works of power, then gifts of healing, helps, administrations, various kinds of tongues." A study of these two verses makes it clear that the gifted *ministers* of verse 28 are the *members* of verse 27, and that the *Church* of verse 28 is the *Body* of verse 27; therefore, what ministers are to the Church, members are to the Body. They hold their position in the Body on account of their functions (the "hearing" and "smelling" of verse 17). The gifted ministers are the functioning members of the Body, and all their operations are as members. They are to the Church what hands, feet, mouth, and head are to the physical body. God's servants do not minister to the Church as apart from it, but as its members. They are *in* the Body, serving it by the use of those faculties which they, as members, possess. A church in any locality is an expression of the one life of the Body, while its ministers are the expression of the difference and yet oneness of its ministry.

First Corinthians 12 deals with the subject of the Body

of Christ, not in its life aspect but in its work aspect. The whole chapter is taken up with the question of ministry, and that ministry is spoken of as the functioning of the different members, from which it is evident that in the thought of God all ministry is on Body ground. Ministry is the practical expression of the Body, an expression of the diversity in unity of its various members. Therefore, we see that when the life aspect of the Body of Christ is expressed, there you have a local church; and when the work aspect is expressed, there you have a manifestation of the gifts God has given to His Church.

In reading 1 Corinthians 12:28 one cannot but be arrested by the striking difference between the description of the first three gifts and the remaining five. Paul, under the inspiration of the Spirit, takes special care in enumerating them—"first apostles, second prophets, third teachers." The first three are specifically numbered, but not the rest; and they are quite distinct in their nature as well as in their numbering. They are men; the rest are things. The three first-named gifts of the Lord to His Church—apostles, prophets, and teachers—stand apart from all the others. They are ministers of God's Word, and their function, to edify the Body of Christ, is the most important function in the Church. *They are the representatives of the ministry of the Body.*

The only scriptural record of the sending forth of apostles is found in Acts 13, and there we see that it is the prophets and teachers who set them apart for their ministry. Scripture provides no precedent for the separation and sending forth of men by one or more individuals, or by any mission or organization; even the sending out of workers by a local church is a thing unknown in the Word of God. The only example provided us there is the separating and sending forth of apostles by the prophets and teachers.

What is the significance of this? In Antioch the prophets and teachers were chosen of God to separate Barnabas and Saul for His service, because they were the ministering members of the church, and this separation of the apostles was *a question of ministry rather than of life.* Had it related to life, and not specifically to service, then it would have been the concern of the whole local church, not merely of its ministering members. But let it be noted that, though Barnabas and Saul were not separated for the work by the entire church, they were sent out not as representatives of a few select members, but as representatives of the whole Body. Their being separated by the prophets and teachers implied that they did not go out on individualistic lines, or on the basis of any organization, but on the ground of the ministry of the Body. The emphasis, as we have seen, was on ministry, not on life, but it was a ministry representing the whole church, not representing any particular section of it. This is clearly expressed by the laying on of hands.

As we have seen, the laying on of hands speaks of oneness (Lev. 1:4), and the only oneness known among the children of God is the oneness of the Body of Christ; therefore, in laying hands upon the apostles, the prophets and teachers definitely stood on the ground of the Body, acting as its representative members. Their action identified the whole church with the apostles, and identified the apostles with the whole church. These prophets and teachers did not stand on individual ground to send the apostles forth as their personal representatives, nor did they stand on the ground of any select company to send them out as representatives of that particular company; but they stood on the ground of the Body, as its ministering members, and set these two apart for the work of the gospel. In their turn the two, being thus separated, went forth, not to represent any particular individuals or any special organization, but to represent the Body of Christ, and the Body of Christ alone. All work that is truly scriptural and truly spiritual must be out from the Body and must minister to the Body. The Body must be the ground on which the worker stands, and it alone must be the sphere in which he works.

On two different occasions Paul had the laying on of hands; first when he believed on the Lord (Acts 9:17), then on the occasion under consideration, when he was sent out from Antioch. The former expressed his identification with the life of the Body; the latter his identification with the ministry of the Body. The first proclaimed him a member of the Body by receiving life from the Head; the second proclaimed him a ministering member, working not as an isolated individual, but in relation to the other members, as a part of one great whole.

In sending Barnabas and Saul from Antioch, the prophets and teachers stood for no "church" or mission; they represented the ministry of the Body. They were not the whole Church; they were only a group of God's servants. They bore no special name, they were bound by no particular organization, and they were subject to no fixed rules. They simply submitted themselves to the control of the Spirit and separated those whom *He* had separated for the work to which *He* had called them. They themselves were not the Body, but they stood on the ground of the Body, under the authority of the Head. Under that authority, and on that ground, they separated men to be apostles; and under the same authority, and on the same ground, others can do the same. The separation of apostles on this principle will mean that the men sent out may differ, those who send them may differ, and the time and place of their sending may differ too; but since all is under the direction of the one Head, and on the ground of the one Body, there will still be no division. If Antioch sends men out on the basis of the Body, and Jerusalem sends men out on the basis of the Body, there will still be inward oneness despite all outward diversity. How grand it would be if there were no representatives of different earthly bodies, but only representatives of *the* Body, the Body of Christ. If thousands of local churches, with thousands of prophets and teachers, each sent out thousands of different workers, there would be a vast outward diversity, but there could still be perfect inward unity if all were sent out under the direction of the one Head and on the ground of the one Body.

That Christ is the Head of the Church is a recognized fact, but that fact needs emphasis in relation to the ministry as well as to the life of the Church. Christian ministry is the ministry of the whole Church, not merely of one section of it. We must see to it that our work is on no lesser basis than the Body of Christ. Otherwise, we lose the headship of Christ, for Christ is not the Head of any system, or mission, or organization: He is the Head of the Church. If we belong to any human organization, then the divine headship ceases to be expressed in our work.

In Scripture we find no trace of man-made organizations sending out men to preach the gospel. We only find representatives of the ministry of the Church, under the guidance of the Spirit and on the ground of the Body, sending out those whom the Spirit has already separated for the work. If those responsible for the sending out of workers sent them out, not as their own representatives or the representatives of any organization, but only as representatives of the Body of Christ, and if those sent out stood on the ground of no particular "church" or mission, but on the ground of *the* Church alone, then no matter from what places the workers came or to what places they went, cooperation and unity would always be possible and much confusion in the work would be avoided.

THEIR MOVEMENTS

After the apostles were called by the Spirit and were separated for the work by the representative members of the Body, what did they do? We need to recall that those who separated them only expressed identification and sympathy by the laying on of hands; they had no authority to control the apostles. Those prophets and teachers at the base assumed no official responsibility in regard to their movements, their methods of work, or the supply of their financial needs. In Scripture we nowhere find that apostles are under the control of any individual or any organized company. They had no regulations to adhere to and no superiors to obey. The Holy Spirit called them, and they followed His leading and guidance; He alone was their Director.

In Acts 13 and 14 we find the first scriptural record of missionary movements. Though today the places we visit and the conditions we meet may be vastly different from those of the Scripture record, yet in principle the experience of the first apostles may well serve as our example. Let us glance for a moment at these two chapters.

32   THE NORMAL CHRISTIAN CHURCH LIFE

"They then, having been sent out by the Holy Spirit, went down to Seleucia; and from there they sailed away to Cyprus. And when they were in Salamis, they announced the word of God in the synagogues of the Jews. And they also had John as their attendant. And when they had passed through the whole island as far as Paphos, they found a certain man, a magician" (13:4-6). From the very outset constant movement characterized those sent ones. A true apostle is a traveler, not a settler.

"And putting out to sea from Paphos, Paul and his companions came to Perga of Pamphylia; and John departed from them and returned to Jerusalem. And they passed through from Perga and arrived at Pisidian Antioch. And they went into the synagogue on the Sabbath day and sat down" (13:13-14). (The Antioch mentioned here is not the same as the Antioch from which Barnabas and Saul set forth on their first missionary tour.) The apostles were constantly on the move, proclaiming the Word of God wherever they went, but until they reached Antioch in Pisidia we are not told anything of the result of their labors. From this point there is a definite development in the work.

"And when the synagogue gathering had been dismissed, many of the Jews and the devout proselytes followed Paul and Barnabas, who spoke to them and urged them to continue in the grace of God" (13:43). Here is the outcome of a short period of witness in Antioch of Pisidia—many of the Jews and religious proselytes believed. A week later almost the whole city gathered together to hear the Word (v. 44), but this enthusiastic response on the part of the people provoked the Jews to jealousy, and they opposed the apostles (v. 45). At this point the apostles turned to the Gentiles (v. 46), and "as many as were appointed to eternal life believed" (v. 48). On the previous Sabbath a number of Jews had received the Word of life. This Sabbath a number of Gentiles believed on the Lord. So not long after the arrival of the apostles in Antioch of Pisidia we find a church there.

But the apostles did not argue, "Now we have a group of believers here. We must stay awhile and shepherd them." They founded a local church at Antioch of Pisidia, but they did not stay to build it up. On they went again, publishing the Word of the Lord "through the whole region" (v. 49). Their objective was not one city, but "all the region." The modern custom of settling down in one place to shepherd a particular flock has no precedent in Scripture.

Persecution followed (v. 50). The opponents of the gospel message expelled the apostles from their coasts, and they answered by shaking the dust from their feet (v. 51). Many a present-day missionary has no dust to shake from his feet! But those who gather no dust lack the characteristic of an apostle. The early apostles never settled down in comfortable homes, nor did they stop for long to pastor the churches they founded. They were constantly traveling. To be an apostle means to be a sent one, that is, to be always going out. A stationary apostle is a contradiction in terms. A true apostle is one who in times of persecution will always have dust to shake off his feet.

What effect had this early departure of the apostles upon the infant church? Here was a group of new believers, mere babes in Christ, and their fathers in the faith forsook them in their infancy. Did they argue, "Why should the apostles be afraid of persecution and leave us to face the opposition alone?" Did they plead with the apostles to remain awhile and care for their spiritual welfare? Did they reason, "If you leave us now we shall be as sheep without a shepherd. If both of you cannot stay, surely one at least can remain behind and look after us. The persecution is so intense, we shall never get through without your help." How amazing the Scripture record is: "And the disciples were filled with joy and with the Holy Spirit" (v. 52).

There was no mourning among the disciples when the apostles left, but great gladness. The disciples were glad, for they knew the Lord; and they might well rejoice, because the apostles' departure meant an opportunity for others to hear the gospel. What was loss to them was gain to Iconium. Those believers were not like the believers of today, hoping for a settled pastor to instruct them, solve their problems, and shelter them from trouble. And those apostles were not like the apostles of today; they were pioneers, not settlers. They did not wait till believers were mature before they left them. They dared to leave them in mere infancy, for they believed in *the power of the life of God* within them.

But those disciples were not only filled with joy; they were filled with the Holy Spirit. The apostles might go, but the Spirit remained. Had the apostles remained to pastor them, it would have mattered little whether they were filled with the Spirit or not. If they had had a pastor to throw light on all their problems, they would have felt little need of the Spirit's instruction; and they would have felt little need of His power if they had had one in their midst who was bearing all responsibility for the spiritual side of the work while they attended to the secular. In Scripture there is not the slightest hint that apostles should settle down to pastor those they have led to the Lord. There are pastors in Scripture, but they are simply brethren raised up of God from *among* the local saints to care for their fellow believers. One of the reasons why so many present-day converts are not filled with the Spirit is that the apostles settle down to shepherd them and take upon themselves the responsibility that belongs to the Holy Spirit.

Praise God that the apostles moved on to Iconium, for "a great multitude of both Jews and Greeks believed" (14:1). Before long "the multitude of the city was divided, and some were with the Jews and some with the apostles" (v. 4). The saved were obviously a great multitude, since their coming out from the unsaved so vitally affected the place as to cause a division in the city. Only a short time after the apostles left Antioch in Pisidia, there was a church established in Iconium; and here, as in the previous place, opposition was intense. The apostles might well have argued that to leave a great multitude of mere babes in Christ exposed to fierce persecution was heartless, and bad policy besides. But the apostles were true to their apostolic calling, and off they went "to the cities of Lycaonia, Lystra and Derbe" (v. 6). And what did they do when they came to Lystra? As elsewhere, so here, "they announced the gospel" (v. 7), and as elsewhere, so here, there was opposition and persecution (v. 19). It is difficult to estimate the number of believers at Lystra,

SEPARATION AND MOVEMENTS OF THE APOSTLES   35

but judging by the remark that the disciples surrounded Paul (v. 20), there must have been at least half a dozen, and there may have been scores or even hundreds. So now there is a church in Lystra!

Does Paul stay to shepherd them awhile, or at least to tend them till the fierceness of the opposition has subsided? No! "On the next day he went out with Barnabas to Derbe" (v. 20). And there again the glad tidings are proclaimed and many disciples are made (v. 21). So another church is formed! And with the founding of a church in Derbe the first missionary tour of the apostles closes.

Looking back over these two chapters, we note that a fundamental principle governs the movements of the apostles. They travel from place to place, according to the leading of the Spirit, preaching the gospel and founding churches. Nowhere do we find them settling down to shepherd and instruct the converts, or to bear any local responsibility in the churches they have founded. In days of peace the apostles were on the move, and in days of persecution likewise. "Go!" was the word of the Lord, and "Go!" was the watchword of the apostles. The outstanding trait of a sent one is that he is always on the move.

ON THEIR RETURN

But the question arises, How were these new converts shepherded and instructed? How were the newly-founded churches established? In studying the Word we find that the missionary tour of the apostles consisted of an outward and a return journey. On their outward journey their first concern was to found churches. On their return journey their chief business was to build them up.

Having "made a considerable number of disciples, they returned to Lystra and to Iconium and to Antioch, establishing the souls of the disciples, exhorting them to continue in the faith and saying that through many tribulations we must enter into the kingdom of God" (14:21-22) Here we see Paul and Barnabas returning to do some construction work in the churches already founded; but as before on their outward journey, so now on their return, they never settle down in any one place.

It is clear then that the apostles did not just move from place to place founding churches; they also did definite construction work. Merely to found churches without establishing them would be like leaving newborn babes to their own resources. The point to note here is that, while the instruction of the new converts and the building up of the churches was a very vital part of the apostles' work, they did it, not by settling down in one place, but rather by *visiting the places* where they had been before. Neither in their initial work of preaching the gospel, nor in their subsequent work of establishing the churches, did the apostles take up their permanent abode in any one place.

Before they left a place where a church had been founded and some construction work done, they appointed elders to bear responsibility there (14:23). This is one of the most important parts of an apostle's work. (This subject will be dealt with more fully in a subsequent chapter.)

Thus the early apostles worked, and the blessing of the Lord rested on their labors. We shall do well if we follow in their steps, but we must realize clearly that even though we adopt apostolic methods, unless we have apostolic consecration, apostolic faith, and apostolic power, we shall still fail to see apostolic results. We dare not underestimate the value of apostolic methods—they are absolutely essential if we are to have apostolic fruits—but we must not overlook the need of apostolic spirituality, and we must not fear apostolic persecution.

BACK TO ANTIOCH

"And from there they sailed away to Antioch, where they had been commended to the grace of God for the work which they fulfilled. And when they arrived and gathered the church together, they declared the things that God had done with them and that He had opened a door of faith to the Gentiles" (14:26-27). On their return to Antioch the apostles "declared the things that God had done with them." It was from Antioch that Paul and Barnabas had gone out, so it was only fitting that on their return they should give an account of the Lord's dealings with them to those from whom they had gone forth. To give reports of the work to those who are truly bearing the burden with us, is sanctioned by God's Word. It is not only permissible, but necessary, that the children of God at the base should be informed of His doings on the field; but we do well to make sure that our reports are not in the nature of advertisements.

In the matter of reporting, we should on the one hand avoid all unnatural reticence and soulish seclusiveness; on the other hand, we must carefully guard against the intrusion of any personal interest. In all reports of the work our aim should be to glorify God and bring spiritual enrichment to those who share them. To utilize reports as a means of propaganda, with material returns in view, is base in the extreme, and unworthy of any Christian. When the motive is to glorify God and benefit His children, but at the same time to make known the needs of the work with a view to receiving material help, it is still far from acceptable to the Lord, and is unworthy of His servants. Our aim should be this alone—that God shall be glorified and His children blessed. If there were this perfect purity of motive in our reports, how differently many of them would be worded!

Each time we write or speak of our work, let us ask ourselves these questions: (1) Am I reporting with a view to gaining publicity for myself and my work? (2) Am I reporting with the double object of glorifying the Lord *and* advertising the work? (3) Am I reporting with this aim *alone,* that God shall be glorified and His children blessed? May the Lord give us grace to report with unmixed motives and perfect purity of heart!

CHAPTER THREE

THE ELDERS APPOINTED BY THE APOSTLES

"Elders" is a designation of Old Testament origin. We find reference made in the Old Testament to the elders of Israel and also to the elders of different cities. In the Gospels we meet the term again, but still in relation to the Israelites. Even the elders referred to in the first part of Acts are of the Old Testament order (4:5, 8, 23; 6:12).

When were elders first instituted in the Church? Acts 11:30 refers to them in connection with the church in Jerusalem, and this is the first mention of elders in connection with any church; but though their existence is mentioned, nothing is said of their origin. Not till Acts 14:23, when we read of Paul and Barnabas returning from their first missionary journey, do we discover who they were, how they were appointed, and by whom. "When they had appointed elders for them in every church and had prayed with fastings, they committed them to the Lord."

THE APPOINTMENT

We have seen that the apostles themselves could not remain with the new believers to shepherd them and to bear the responsibility of the work locally. How then were the new converts cared for, and how was the work carried on? The apostles did not request that men be sent from Antioch to shepherd the flocks, nor did one of them remain behind to bear the burden of the local churches. What they did was simply this: "When they had appointed elders for them in every church and had prayed with fastings, they committed them to the Lord into whom they had believed" (v. 23). Wherever a church had been founded on their outward journey, they appointed elders on their return journey. They did not wait until any arbitrary standard was reached before appointing elders in a church, but "in every church" they chose a few of the more mature members to care for their fellow believers.

The apostolic procedure was quite simple. The apostles visited a place, founded a church, left that church for a while, then returned to establish it. In the interval certain developments would naturally take place. When the apostles left, some of the professing believers would leave too. Others would continue to attend the meetings, and would prove themselves to be truly the Lord's, but would make no appreciable progress. Others again would eagerly press on in the knowledge of the Lord and show real concern for His interests. Those who had more spiritual life than others would spontaneously come to the front and take responsibility for their weaker brethren. It was because they had proved themselves to be elders that the apostles appointed them to hold office as elders, and it was their business to shepherd and instruct the other believers, and to superintend and control the church affairs.

Nowhere did the apostles settle down and assume responsibility for the local church, but in every church they founded they chose from *among* the local believers faithful ones upon whom such responsibility could be placed. When they had chosen elders in each church, with prayer and fasting they committed them to the Lord, just as, with prayer and fasting, they themselves had been committed to the Lord by the prophets and teachers when they were sent out on their apostolic ministry. If this committal of elders to the Lord is to be of spiritual value, and no mere official ceremony, a vital knowledge of the Lord will be required on the part of the apostles. It is easy to become so occupied with the problems and needs of the situation, that one instinctively takes the burden upon oneself, even while admitting the truth that the Lord is responsible for His own Church. We need to know Christ as Head of His Church in no mere intellectual way if we are to let all its management pass out of our hands at the very outset. Only an utter distrust of themselves, and a living trust in God, could enable the early apostles to commit the affairs of every local church into the hands of local men who had but recently come to know the Lord. All who are engaged in apostolic work, and are seeking to follow the example of the first apostles in leaving the churches to the management of local elders, must be spiritually equipped for the task; for if things pass out of human hands and are not committed in faith to divine hands, the result will be disaster. Oh, how we need a living faith and a living knowledge of the living God!

The Word of God makes it clear that the oversight of a church is not the work of apostles, but of elders. Although Paul stayed in Corinth for over a year, in Rome for two years, and in Ephesus for three years, yet in none of these places did he assume responsibility for the work of the local church. In Scripture we read of the elders of Ephesus, but never of the apostles *of* Ephesus. We find no mention made of the apostles *of* Philippi, but we do find reference to the bishops of Philippi. Apostles are responsible for their own particular ministry, but not for the churches which are the fruit of their ministry. All the fruit of the apostles' work had to be handed over to the care of local elders.

In God's plan provision has been made for the building up of local churches, and in that plan pastors have a place, but it was never His thought that apostles should assume the role of pastors. He purposed that apostles should be responsible for the work in *different* places, while elders were to bear responsibility in *one* place. The characteristic of an apostle is *going;* the characteristic of an elder is *staying*. It is not necessary that elders resign their ordinary professions and devote themselves exclusively to their duties in connection with the church. They are simply *local* men, following their usual pursuits and at the same time bearing special responsibilities in the church. Should local affairs increase, they may devote themselves entirely to spiritual work, but the characteristic of an elder is not that he is a "full-time Christian worker." It is merely that, as a local brother, he bears responsibility in the local church. Locality determines the boundary of a church, and it is for that reason that the elders are always chosen from among the more mature believers in any place, and not transferred from other places. Thus, the local character of the churches of God is preserved, and consequently also their independent government and spiritual unity.

According to the usual conception of things, one would think it necessary for a considerable time to elapse between the founding of a church and the appointment of elders, but that is not according to God's pattern. The first missionary tour of the apostles covered less than two years, and during that period the apostles preached the gospel, led sinners to the Lord, formed churches, and appointed elders wherever a church had been formed. The elders were chosen on the apostles' return journey, not on their first visit to any place; but the interval between their two visits was never long, at the most a matter of months. On their return journey the apostles would naturally find some places progressing more favorably than others, but they did not reason that, because of the low state of any church, they would make an exception and appoint no elders. They appointed elders in every church. Some may ask, If all the members of a church are in a low spiritual condition, how is it possible to appoint elders among them? It may solve the problem of many if they only consider the implication of the term "elder." The existence of an elder implies the existence of a junior. The word "elder" is relative, not absolute. Among a group of men in their seventy-ninth year it takes a man in his eightieth year to be their elder; but it only takes a child of eight to be "elder" to a company of children of seven. Even among the spiritually immature there are bound to be those who, in comparison with the others, are more mature and have spiritual possibilities, which is all the qualification they require to be their elders.

A church may come far short of the ideal, but we cannot on that account deprive it of the status of a church. Our responsibility is to minister to it and so seek to bring it nearer the ideal. In the same way, even the comparatively advanced ones in a locality may not reach the ideal of elders, but we cannot for that reason deprive them of the status of elders. In comparison with the elders of other places they may seem

THE ELDERS APPOINTED BY THE APOSTLES

very immature, but if they are more advanced than the other believers in the same locality, then in their own church they *are* elders. We must remember that the office of an elder according to Scripture is limited to a locality. Being an elder in Nanking does not qualify a man to be an elder in Shanghai; but even if his spiritual state is far from what it should be, provided he is in advance of his fellow believers in the same church, then he is qualified to be an elder there. You can only have pattern elders where you have a pattern church. Where a church is immature, the elders will naturally be immature; where a church is mature, the elders will also be mature. The model elders of 1 Timothy 3 and of Titus 1 are to be found in model churches.

The appointing of comparatively spiritual brothers to be elders is a principle set forth in the Word of God, though it runs counter to the modern conception of things. But even while we recognize this principle, we must not seek to apply it in any legal way. That would spell death. We must force nothing, but must be continually open to the leading of the Spirit. He will indicate the right time for the appointment of elders in any church. Should there be no leading of the Holy Spirit, and circumstances not permit an immediate appointment of elders on the second visit of the apostles, then a Titus could be left behind to see to their appointment later. This is the first subject dealt with in the book of Titus, and it is a most important one. Paul gives Titus injunctions to establish elders in every city in Crete (Titus 1:5).

In the appointment of elders the apostles did not follow their personal preferences; they only appointed those whom God had already chosen. That is why Paul could say to the elders in Ephesus, "The Holy Spirit has placed you as overseers" (Acts 20:28). The apostles did not take the initiative in the matter. They merely established as elders those whom the Holy Spirit *had already* made overseers in the church. In a man-made organization the appointment of an individual to office entitles him to occupy that office; but not so in the Church of God. Everything there is on a spiritual basis, and it is only divine appointment that qualifies a man for office. If the Holy Spirit does not make men bishops, then no apostolic appointment will ever avail to do so. In the Church of God everything is under the sovereignty of the Spirit; man is ruled out. Elders are not men who think themselves capable to control church affairs, or men whom the apostles consider suitable, but men whom the *Holy Spirit* has set to be overseers in the Church. Those whom the Spirit chooses to be shepherds of the flock, to them He also gives grace and gifts to qualify them for spiritual leadership. It is their spiritual call and their spiritual equipment, not their official appointment, that constitutes them elders. In a spiritual sense they are already elders before they hold the position officially, and it is because they actually *are* elders that they are publicly appointed to be elders. In the early Church it was the Holy Spirit who first signified His choice of elders; then the apostles confirmed the choice by appointing them to office.

APOSTLES AND ELDERS

Elders were local men appointed to oversee affairs in the local church. Their sphere of office was limited by the locality. An elder in Ephesus was not an elder in Smyrna, and an elder in Smyrna was not an elder in Ephesus. In Scripture there are no local apostles, nor are there any extra-local elders; all elders are local, and all apostles are extra-local. The Word of God nowhere speaks of apostles managing the affairs of a local church, and it nowhere speaks of elders managing the affairs of several local churches. The apostles were the ministers of all the churches, but they had control of none. The elders were confined to one church, and they controlled affairs in that one. The duty of apostles was to found churches. Once a church was established, all responsibility was handed over to the local elders, and from that day the apostles exercised no control whatever in its affairs. All management was in the hands of the elders, and if they thought it right, they could even refuse an apostle entry into their church. Should such a thing occur, the apostle would have no authority to insist on being received, since all local authority had already passed from his hands into the hands of the elders.

How did Paul deal with the adulterous believer in Corinth?

THE ELDERS APPOINTED BY THE APOSTLES 45

He did not just notify the church that he had excommunicated the man. The utmost he could do was to instruct its members regarding the seriousness of the situation and seek to admonish them to remove the wicked person from their midst (1 Cor. 5:13). If the church was right spiritually they would pay attention to Paul, but if they disregarded his exhortations, while they would be wrong spiritually, they would not be wrong legally. In the event of their despising his counsel, Paul could only bring his spiritual authority to bear on the situation. In the name of the Lord Jesus he could "deliver such a one to Satan for the destruction of his flesh" (v. 5). He had no official authority to discipline him, but he had spiritual authority to deal with the case. He had his spiritual "rod."

The affairs of the local church are entirely independent of the apostles. Once elders have been appointed, all control passes into their hands, and while thereafter an apostle may still instruct and persuade, he can never interfere. But this did not hinder Paul from speaking authoritatively to the Corinthians. Even a casual reader will notice how authoritative his statements were in both Epistles. It was quite within his province to pass judgment where doctrinal and moral questions were concerned, and when Paul did so he was most emphatic; but the actual enforcing of such judgments was outside his province and entirely a matter for the local church.

An apostle can deal with the disorders of a church whenever his advice and counsel are sought, as was the case with Paul and the church in Corinth. It was because of their inquiries that he could say to them, "And the rest I will set in order when I come" (1 Cor. 11:34). But the point to note here is that the rest of the matters which Paul intended to set in order on his arrival in Corinth were to be attended to in the same way as those he had dealt with in his Epistle, and they were dealt with *doctrinally.* In like manner as he had instructed them concerning certain affairs there, so he would instruct them concerning the remaining matters on his arrival; but the Corinthians themselves, not Paul, were the ones who would have *to deal* with the situation.

Since Peter and John were apostles, how did it come about

that they were elders of the church in Jerusalem? (1 Pet. 5:1; 2 John 1; 3 John 1). They were elders as well as apostles because they were not only responsible for the work in different places, but also for the church in *their own* place. When they went out, they ministered in the capacity of apostles, bearing the responsibility for the work in other parts. When they returned home, they performed the duties of elders, bearing the responsibility of the local church. (Only such apostles as are not traveling *much* could be elders of the church in their own locality.) When Peter and John were away from their own church, they were apostles; when they returned, they were elders. It was not on the ground of their being apostles that they were elders in Jerusalem; they were elders there solely on the ground of their being local men of greater spiritual maturity than their brethren.

There is no precedent in Scripture for a *visiting* apostle to settle down as elder in any church he visits; but, provided circumstances permit him to be at home frequently, he could be an elder in his own locality, on the ground of his being a local brother. If the local character of the churches of God is to be preserved, then the extra-local character of the apostles must also be preserved.

Paul was sent out from Antioch, and he founded a church in Ephesus. We know he did not hold the office of elder in any church, but it would have been possible for him to be an elder in Antioch, not in Ephesus. He spent three years in Ephesus, but he worked there in the capacity of an apostle, not an elder; that is, he assumed no responsibility and exercised no authority in local affairs, but simply devoted himself to his apostolic ministry. Let us note carefully that *there are no elders in the universal Church and no apostles in the local church.*

THEIR RESPONSIBILITIES

It is the responsibility of every saved man to serve the Lord according to his capacity and in his own sphere. God did not appoint elders to do the work on behalf of their brethren. After the appointment of elders, as before, it is still the brethren's duty and privilege to serve the Lord. Elders are also called bishops (Acts 20:28; Titus 1:5, 7). The term "elder" relates to their person; the term "bishop" to their work. Bishop means overseer, and an overseer is not one who works instead of others, but one who supervises others as they work. God intended that every Christian should be a "Christian worker," and He appointed some to take the oversight of the work so that it might be carried on efficiently. It was never His thought that the majority of the believers should devote themselves exclusively to secular affairs and leave the church matters to a group of spiritual specialists. This point cannot be overemphasized. Elders are not a group of men who contract to do the church work on behalf of its members; they are only the ones who superintend affairs. It is their business to encourage the backward and restrain the forward ones, never doing the work instead of them, but simply directing them in the doing of it.

The responsibility of an elder relates to matters temporal and spiritual. They are appointed to "lead," and also to "instruct" and "shepherd." "Let the elders who take the lead well be counted worthy of double honor, especially those who labor in word and teaching" (1 Tim. 5:17). "Shepherd the flock of God among you, overseeing not under compulsion but willingly, according to God; not by seeking gain through base means but eagerly; nor as lording it over your allotments but by becoming patterns of the flock" (1 Pet. 5:2-3).

The Word of God uses the term "lead" in connection with the responsibilities of an elder. The ordering of church government, the management of business affairs, and the care of material things are all under their control. But we must remember that a scriptural church does not consist of an active and a passive group of brethren, the former controlling the latter, and the latter simply submitting to their control, or the former bearing all the burden while the latter settle down in ease to enjoy the benefit of their labors. "That the members would...care for one another" is God's purpose for His Church (1 Cor. 12:25). Every church after God's own heart bears the stamp of "one another" on all its life and activity. Mutuality is its outstanding characteristic. If the elders lose sight of that, then their leading the church will soon be changed to *lording* it over the church. Even while the elders exercise control in church affairs, they must remember that they are only fellow members with the other believers; Christ alone is the Head. They were not appointed to be lords of their brethren, but to be their *examples*. What is an example? It is a pattern for others to follow. Since they were to be a pattern to the brethren, then obviously it was neither God's thought for them to do all the work and the brethren none, nor for the brethren to do the work while they simply stood by and commanded. For the elders to be a pattern to the brethren implied that the brethren worked and the elders worked as well. It also implied that the elders worked with special diligence and care, so that the brethren should have a good example to follow. They were overseers, but they were not lords of their brethren, standing aloof and commanding; *and* they did direct the work, but they did it more by example than by command. Such is the scriptural conception of the leading of the elders.

But their responsibility does not merely relate to the material side of church affairs. If God has equipped them with spiritual gifts, then they should also bear spiritual responsibility. Paul wrote to Timothy, "Let the elders who take the lead well be counted worthy of double honor, especially those who labor in word and teaching" (1 Tim. 5:17). It is the responsibility of all elders to control the affairs of the church, but such as have special gifts (as of prophecy or teaching) are free to exercise these for the spiritual edification of the church. Paul wrote to Titus that an elder should "be able both to exhort by the healthy teaching and to convict those who oppose" (Titus 1:9). The preaching and teaching in the local church is not the business of apostles but of local brethren who are in the ministry, especially if they are elders. As we have already seen, the management of a church is a matter of local responsibility; so also is teaching and preaching.

On the spiritual side of the work the elders help to build up the church not only by teaching and preaching, but by pastoral work. To shepherd the flock is particularly the work of elders. Paul said to the Ephesian elders, "Take heed to yourselves and to all the flock, among whom the Holy Spirit has placed you as overseers to shepherd the church of God" (Acts 20:28). And Peter wrote in the same strain to the elders among the saints of the Dispersion, "Shepherd the flock of God among you" (1 Pet. 5:2). The present-day conception of pastors is far removed from the thought of God. God's thought was that men chosen *from among the local brethren* should shepherd the flock, not that men coming from other parts should preach the gospel, found churches, and then settle down to care for those churches. A clear understanding of the respective responsibilities of apostles and elders would clear away many of the difficulties that exist in the church today.

THE PLURALITY OF ELDERS

This work of leading, teaching, and shepherding the flock, which we have seen to be the special duty of the elders, does not devolve upon one man only in any place. To have pastors in a church is scriptural, but the present-day pastoral system is quite unscriptural; it is an invention of man.

In Scripture we see that there was always more than one elder or bishop in a local church. It is not God's will that one believer should be singled out from all the others to occupy a place of special prominence, while the others passively submit to his will. If the management of the entire church rests upon one man, how easy it is for him to become self-conceited, esteeming himself above measure and suppressing the other brethren (3 John). God has ordained that several elders together share the work of the church, so that no one individual should be able to run things according to his own pleasure, treating the church as his own special property and leaving the impress of his personality upon all its life and work. To place the responsibility in the hands of several brethren, rather than in the hands of one individual, is God's way of safeguarding His church against the evils that result from the domination of a strong personality. God has purposed that several brothers should unitedly bear responsibility in the church, so that even in controlling its affairs they have to depend one upon the other and submit one to the other. Thus, in an experimental way, they will discover the meaning of bearing the cross, and they will have opportunity to give practical expression to the truth of the Body of Christ. As they honor one another and trust one another to the leading of the Spirit, none taking the place of the Head, but each regarding the others as fellow members, the element of mutuality, which is the distinctive feature of the church, will be preserved.

Chapter Four

THE CHURCHES FOUNDED BY THE APOSTLES

THE CHURCH AND THE CHURCHES

The Word of God teaches us that the Church is one. Why then did the apostles found separate churches in each of the places they visited? If the *Church* is the Body of Christ, it cannot but be one. Then how does it come about that we speak of *churches?*

The word "church" means "the called-out ones." The term is used twice in the Gospels, once in Matthew 16:18 and once in Matthew 18:17, and we meet in quite frequently in the Acts and the Epistles. In the Gospels the word is used on both occasions by our Lord, but it is employed in a somewhat different sense each time.

"You are Peter, and upon this rock I will build My church, and the gates of Hades shall not prevail against it" (Matt. 16:18). What church is this? Peter confessed that Jesus was the Christ, the Son of the living God, and our Lord declared that He would build His Church upon this confession—the confession that as to His Person He is the Son of God, and as to His work He is the Christ of God. This Church comprises all the saved, without reference to time or space, that is, all who in the purpose of God are redeemed by virtue of the shed blood of the Lord Jesus, and are born again by the operation of His Spirit. This is the Church universal, the Church of God, the Body of Christ.

"And if he refuses to hear them, tell it to the church" (Matt. 18:17). The word "church" is used here in quite a different sense from the sense in Matthew 16:18. The sphere of the church referred to here is clearly not as wide as the sphere of the Church mentioned in the previous passage. The

Church there is a Church that knows nothing of time or place, but the church here is obviously limited both to time and place, for it is one that can hear you speak. The Church mentioned in chapter sixteen includes all the children of God in every locality, while the church mentioned in chapter eighteen includes only the children of God living in one locality; and it is because it is limited to one place that it is possible for you to tell your difficulties to the believers of whom it is composed. Obviously the church here is local, not universal, for no one could speak at one time to all the children of God throughout the universe. It is only possible to speak at one time to the believers living in one place.

We have clearly two different aspects of the Church before us—the Church and the churches, the universal Church and the local churches. The Church is invisible; the churches are visible. The Church has no organization; the churches are organized. The Church is spiritual; the churches are spiritual and yet physical. The Church is purely an organism; the churches are an organism, yet at the same time they are organized, which is seen by the fact that elders and deacons hold office there.[1]

All Church difficulties arise in connection with the local churches, not with the universal Church. The latter is invisible and spiritual, therefore beyond the reach of man, while the former is visible and organized, therefore still liable to be touched by human hands. The heavenly Church is so far removed from the world that it is possible to remain unaffected by it, but the earthly churches are so close to us, that if problems arise there we feel them acutely. The invisible church does not test our obedience to God, but the visible churches test us severely by facing us with issues on the intensely practical plane of our earthly life.

THE BASIS OF THE CHURCHES

In the Word of God we find "the church of God" spoken of in the singular (1 Cor. 10:32), but we find the same Word

---

[1] Throughout this book it would be well for the reader to distinguish clearly between the Church and the church.

referring to the "churches of God" in the plural (1 Thes. 2:14). How has this unity become a plurality? How has the Church which is essentially one become many? The Church of God has been divided into the churches of God on the one ground of difference of locality.[1] Locality is the only scriptural basis for the division of the Church into churches.

The seven churches in Asia, referred to in the book of Revelation, comprised the church in Ephesus, the church in Smyrna, the church in Pergamos, the church in Thyatira, the church in Sardis, the church in Philadelphia, and the church in Laodicea. They were seven churches, not one. Each was distinct from the others on the ground of the difference of locality. It was only because the believers did not reside in one place that they did not belong to one church. There were seven different churches simply because the believers lived in seven different places. Ephesus, Smyrna, Pergamos, Thyatira, Sardis, Philadelphia, and Laodicea are clearly all the names of places. Not only were the seven churches in Asia founded on the basis of locality, but all the churches mentioned in Scripture were founded on the same basis. Throughout the Word of God we can find no name attached to a church save the name of a place, for example, the church in Jerusalem, the church in Lystra, the church in Derbe, the church in Colosse, the church in Troas, the church in Thessalonica, the church in Antioch. This fact cannot be overemphasized, that *in Scripture no other name but the name of a locality is ever connected with a church, and division of the church into churches is solely on the ground of difference of locality.*

Spiritually the Church of God is one; therefore, it cannot be divided—but physically its members are scattered throughout the earth; therefore, they cannot possibly live in one place.[2] Yet it is essential that there be a physical gathering together of believers. It is not enough that they be present

---

[1] The word "divided" is used here in its purest sense.

[2] The grudge which certain writers bear against the use of the word "member" in connection with the word "church" is merely a matter of terms, not of facts.

"in the spirit"; they must also be present "in the flesh." Now a church is composed of all "the called-out ones assembled" in one place for worship, prayer, fellowship, and ministry. This assembling together is absolutely essential to the life of a church. Without it, there may be believers scattered throughout the area, but there is really no church. *The Church* exists because of the existence of its members, and it does not require that they meet in a physical way; but it is essential to the very existence of *a church* that its members gather together in a physical way. It is in this latter sense that the word "church" is used in 1 Corinthians 14. The phrase "in the church" (vv. 19, 23, 28) means "in the church meetings." A church is a church assembled. These believers are not separated from other believers in any respect but that of their dwelling places. As long as they continue in the flesh, they will be limited by space, and this physical limitation, which in the very nature of things makes it impossible for God's people to meet in one place, is the only basis sanctioned by God for the forming of separate churches. Christians belong to different churches for the sole reason that they live in different places. That division is merely external. In reality the church as the Body of Christ cannot be divided; therefore, even when the Word of God refers to the different assemblies of His people, the places named vary, but it is still "the church" in every one of these places, such as "the church in Ephesus," "the church in Smyrna," "the church in Pergamos."

In the New Testament there is one method and one alone of dividing the Church into churches, and that God-ordained method is division on the basis of locality. All other methods are man-made, not God-given. May the Spirit of God engrave this truth deeply on our hearts, that the only reason for the division of God's children into different churches is because of the different places in which they live.

What is a New Testament church? It is not a building, a gospel hall, a preaching center, a mission, a work, an organization, a system, a denomination, or a sect. People may apply the term "church" to any of the above; nevertheless they are not churches. A New Testament church is the meeting together for worship, prayer, fellowship, and mutual edification, of all the people of God in a given locality, on the ground that they are Christians in the same locality. The Church is the Body of Christ; a church is a miniature Body of Christ. All the believers in a locality form the church in that locality, and in a small way they ought to show forth what the Church should show forth. They are the Body of Christ in that locality, so they have to learn how to come under the headship of the Lord, and how to manifest oneness among all the members, guarding carefully against schism and division.

THE BOUNDARY OF A LOCALITY

We have seen that all the churches in Scripture are local churches, but the question naturally arises, What is a scriptural locality? If we note what places are mentioned in God's Word in connection with the founding of churches, then we shall be able to determine what the extent of a place must be to justify its being regarded as a unit for the forming of a church. In Scripture the localities which determine the boundary of a church are *neither countries, nor provinces, nor districts.* Nowhere do we read of a national church, or a provincial church, or of a district church. We read of the church in Ephesus, the church in Rome, the church in Jerusalem, the church in Corinth, the church in Philippi, and the church in Iconium. Now what kind of places are Ephesus, Rome, Jerusalem, Corinth, Philippi, and Iconium? They are neither countries, nor provinces, nor districts, but simply places of convenient size for people to live together in a certain measure of safety and sociability. In modern language we should call them cities. That cities were the boundaries of churches in the apostolic days is evident from the fact that on the one hand Paul and Barnabas "appointed elders for them in every church" (Acts 14:23), and on the other hand Paul instructed Titus to "appoint elders in every city" (Titus 1:5).

In the Word of God we see no church that extends beyond the area of a city, nor do we find any church which does not cover the entire area. A city is the scriptural unit of locality. From Genesis and Joshua we learn that cities in olden days were the places where people grouped together to live; they were also the smallest unit of civil administration, and each possessed an independent name. Any place is qualified to be a unit for the founding of a church which is a place where people group together to live, a place with an independent name, and a place which is the smallest political unit. Such a place is a scriptural city and is the boundary of a local church. Large cities such as Rome and Jerusalem are only units, while small cities such as Iconium and Troas are likewise units. Apart from such places where people live a community life, there is no scriptural unit of the churches of God.

Questions will naturally arise concerning large cities such as London. Are they counted as one unit-locality, or more than one? London is clearly not a city in the scriptural sense of the term, and it cannot therefore be regarded as a unit. Even people living in London talk about going "into the city," or "into town," which reveals the fact that, in their thinking, London and "the city" are not synonymous. The political and postal authorities, as well as the man on the street, regard London as more than one unit. They divide it respectively into boroughs and postal districts. What they regard as an administrative unit, we may well regard as a church unit.

As to country-places which could not technically be termed cities, they may also be regarded as unit-localities. It is said of our Lord, when on earth, that He went out into the cities and villages (Luke 13:22), from which we see that country-places, as well as towns, are considered to be separate units.

This division of churches according to locality is a demonstration of the marvelous wisdom of God. Had God ordained that the Church be divided into churches with the country as their boundary, then in the event of one country being vanquished and absorbed by another, the church would have to change its sphere. Were a province to mark the limit of a church, the sphere of the churches would be frequently altered because of the frequent change of provincial boundary. The same holds true in respect of a district. The most stable of all political units is a village, a town, or a city. Governments, dynasties, and countries may change, but cities are seldom affected by any political change. There are cities that have passed from one country to another and still have their original name, and there are cities in existence today that have retained the same name for centuries. So we see the divine wisdom in decreeing that a locality should fix the boundary of a church.

Since the limits of a locality mark the limits of a church, then no church can be narrower than a locality, and none wider. The Word of God recognizes only two churches, the universal Church and the local churches; there is no third church whose sphere is narrower than the local, or else wider than the local and yet narrower than the universal Church. A local church admits of no possible division, and it admits of no possible extension. You cannot narrow its sphere by dividing it into several smaller churches, nor can you widen its sphere by linking several local churches together. Any church smaller than a local church is not a scriptural church, and any church larger than a local church, and yet smaller than the universal Church, is not a scriptural church either.

NOT NARROWER THAN A LOCALITY

We read in 1 Corinthians 1:2 of "the church of God which is in Corinth." Corinth was a unit-locality, and the church in Corinth, a unit-church. When discord crept in and its members were on the point of splitting the church into four different factions, Paul wrote, rebuking them: "Each of you says, I am of Paul, and I of Apollos, and I of Cephas, and I of Christ....Are you not men of flesh?" (1 Cor. 1:12; 3:4). Had these people formed four different groups, they would have been sects, not churches, for Corinth was a city, and that is the smallest unit which warrants the forming of a church. The church of God in Corinth could not cover a lesser area than the whole city, nor could it comprise a lesser number of Christians than all the Christians who lived there. This is Paul's definition of the church in Corinth—"to those who have been sanctified in Christ Jesus, the called saints" (1:2). To form a church in an area smaller than a unit-locality is to form it on a smaller basis than a scriptural unit, and it follows that it cannot be a scriptural church. Any group of believers less than all the believers in a place is not qualified to be a separate church. The unit of the church must correspond with the unit of the locality. *A church must cover the same area as the locality in which it is found.* If a church is smaller than a locality, then it is not a scriptural church; it is a sect.

To say, "I am of Paul," or "I am of Cephas," is obviously sectarian; but to say, "I am of Christ," is sectarian too, though less obviously so. The confession, "I am of Christ," is good as a confession, but it is not an adequate basis for forming a separate church, since it excludes some of the children of God in a given locality by including only a certain section who say, "I am of Christ." That every believer belongs to Christ is a fact, whether that fact be declared or not; and to differentiate between those who proclaim it and those who do not, is condemned by God as carnal. It is the fact that matters, not the declaration of it. The sphere of a church in any place does not merely include those in that place who say, "I am of Christ," but all in that place who *are* of Christ. It extends over the entire area of the locality, and includes the entire number of the Christians in the locality.

To take one's stand as belonging to Christ alone is perfectly right, but to divide between Christians who take that stand and Christians who do not, is altogether wrong. To brand as sectarian those who say, "I am of Paul," or "I am of Cephas," and feel spiritually superior as we separate ourselves from them and have fellowship only with those who say, "I am of Christ," makes us guilty of the very sin we condemn in others. If we make non-sectarianism the basis of our fellowship, then we are dividing the church on a ground other than the one ordained of God, and thereby we form another sect. The scriptural ground for a church *is a locality and not non-sectarianism.* Any fellowship that is not as wide as the locality is sectarian. All Christians who live in the same place as I do, are in the same church as I am, and I dare exclude none. I acknowledge as my brother, and as a fellow member of my church, every child of God who lives in my locality.

There were a great number of believers in Jerusalem. We read of a multitude who turned to the Lord; yet they are all referred to as the church in Jerusalem, not the churches in

Jerusalem. Jerusalem was a *single place;* therefore, it could only be counted as a *single unit* for the founding of a single church. You cannot divide the church unless you can divide the place. If there is only one locality, there can only be one church. In Corinth there was only *the* church in Corinth; in Hankow there is only *the* church in Hankow. We do not read of the churches in Jerusalem, or the churches in Ephesus, or the churches in Corinth. Each of these was counted as only one place; therefore, it was permissible to have only one church in each. As long as Jerusalem, Ephesus, and Corinth remain unit-localities, just so long do they remain unit-churches. *If a locality is indivisible, then the church formed in that locality is indivisible.*

NOT WIDER THAN A LOCALITY

We have just seen that the boundary of a church cannot be narrower than the locality to which it belongs. On the other hand, its boundary cannot be wider than the locality. In the Word of God we never read of the church in Macedonia, or the church in Galatia, or the church in Judea, or the church in Galilee. Why? Because Macedonia and Galilee are provinces, and Judea and Galatia are districts. A province is not a scriptural unit of locality; neither is a district. Both include a number of units; therefore, they include a number of separate churches and do not constitute one church. A provincial church or a district church is not according to Scripture, since it does not divide on the ground of locality, but combines a number of localities. It is because all scriptural churches are local churches that there is no mention of state churches, provincial churches, or district churches in the Word of God.

"Then had the churches rest throughout all Judea and Galilee and Samaria" (Acts 9:31, KJV). The Holy Spirit did not speak here of the church, but of the churches. Because there were a number of localities, there were also a number of churches. It was not God's plan to unite the churches of different places into one church, but to have a separate church in each place. There were as many churches as there were places.

"He passed through Syria and Cilicia, confirming the

churches" (Acts 15:41). Again the reference is not to one single church, because Syria and Cilicia were vast districts, each comprising a number of different places. It is permissible in political circles to unite many different places into a district and call it Syria or Cilicia, but God does not unite the believers in a number of different places and call them the church in Syria, or the church in Cilicia. There may be unions or mergers in the commercial or political world, but God sanctions no combinations among the churches. *Each separate place must have a separate church.*

"All the churches of the Gentiles" (Rom. 16:4). The churches of God were not formed on national lines but on local lines; therefore, there is no mention of the church of the Gentiles, but of the churches of the Gentiles.

"The churches of Asia greet you" (1 Cor. 16:19). "The churches of Macedonia" (2 Cor. 8:1). "The churches of Galatia" (Gal. 1:2). "I was still unknown by face to the churches of Judea, which are in Christ" (Gal. 1:22). Asia, Macedonia, Galatia, and Judea were all areas comprising more than one locality-unit; therefore, the Word of God refers to the churches in these areas. A church according to the divine thought is always a church in one locality; any other kind of church is a product of the human mind.

God sanctions no division of the church within any one locality, and He sanctions no denominational combination of the churches in a number of localities. In Scripture there is always one church in one place, never several churches in one place, nor one church in several places. God does not recognize any fellowship of His children on a basis narrower, or wider, than that of a locality.

Nanking is a city, and so is Soochow. Because each is a separate unit, each therefore has a separate church. The two places are both in the same country, and even in the same province, but because they are two separate cities, they must form two separate churches. Politically Glasgow and Nanking do not belong to the same province, or even the same country; yet the relationship between Nanking and Soochow is exactly the same as between Nanking and Glasgow. Nanking and Soochow are as truly separate units as Nanking and Glasgow are. In the division of churches the question of country or province does not arise; it is all a question of cities. Two cities of the same country, or the same province, have no closer relationship than two cities of different countries or different provinces. God's intention is that a church in any one locality should be a unit, and in their relationship one to the other the different churches must preserve their local character.

When God's people throughout the earth really see the local character of the churches, then they will appreciate their oneness in Christ as never before. The churches of God are local, *intensely local*. If any factor enters in to destroy their local character, then they cease to be scriptural churches.

THE INDEPENDENCE OF THE CHURCHES

It was never God's purpose that a number of churches in different places should be combined under any denomination or organization, but rather that each one should be independent of the other. Their responsibilities were to be independent and their government likewise. When our Lord sent messages to His children in Asia, He did not address them as "the church in Asia," but "the seven churches which are in Asia." His rebuke of Ephesus could not be applied to Smyrna, because Smyrna was independent of Ephesus. The confusion in Pergamos could not be laid to the charge of Philadelphia, because Philadelphia was independent of Pergamos. And the pride of Laodicea could not be attributed to Sardis, because Sardis was independent of Laodicea. Each church stood on its own merits and bore its own responsibility. Since God's children lived in seven different cities, they consequently belonged to seven different churches. And since each was independent of the other, each had its own special commendation, or exhortation, or rebuke.

And not only were there these seven churches on earth; there were seven lampstands representing them in heaven. In the Old Testament there was only one lampstand with seven different branches, but in the New Testament there were seven distinct lampstands. Had the New Testament representation been the same as the Old, then believers in the seven Asiatic churches might have united to form one church; but there are now seven separate lampstands, each upon its own base, so that the Lord is able to walk "in the midst of the seven golden lampstands" (Rev. 2:1). Therefore, though all churches stand under the authority of the one Head and express the life of the one Body (for they are all made of gold), still they are not united by any outward organization, but each stands on its own base, bearing its own responsibility, maintaining its local independence.

AMONG THE CHURCHES

This does not imply that the different local churches have nothing to do with one another, and that each can simply do as it pleases without considering the rest, for the ground of a church is the ground of the Body. Although they are unit-churches in outward management, still their inner life is one, and the Lord has made their members the members of one Body. There is no outward organization forming them into one big combined unit, but there is a strong inward bond uniting them in the Lord. They have a oneness of life which knows nothing of the bounds of locality, and which leads the separate churches to uniform action despite the absence of all outward organization. In organization the churches are totally independent of one another, but in life they are one, and consequently interdependent. If one church receives revelation, the others should seek to profit by it. If one is in difficulty, the others should come to its aid. But while the churches minister one to the other, they should always preserve their independence of government and responsibility.

On the one hand, each church is directly under the authority of the Lord and responsible to Him alone; on the other hand, each must listen not only to His direct speaking, but to His speaking through the others. "He who has an ear, let him hear what the Spirit says to the churches," is our Lord's injunction to all (Rev. 2 and 3). In the introduction of His letters to the seven churches we find our Lord addressing the angel of each church, but at their close we find that His message to one particular church was also a message to all the churches. From this it is clear that what one church ought to do, all the churches ought to do. The responsibility of the churches is individual, but their actions should be uniform. This balance of truth ought to be carefully preserved.

We find the same teaching in the Epistles. "Because of this I have sent Timothy to you...who will remind you of my ways which are in Christ, even as I teach everywhere in every church" (1 Cor. 4:17). What Paul has taught "everywhere in every church," the Corinthians are called upon to lay to heart. There is not one kind of instruction for Corinth, and another kind of instruction for another place. What the apostles have been teaching to some of the churches, the believers in other churches must also note. And that applies to commandments as well as to matters of doctrine. "As the Lord has apportioned to each one...so let him walk. And so I direct in all the churches" (1 Cor. 7:17). The Lord could never give a command to one church which in any way contradicted His command to another church. His requirements for one group of His children were His requirements for all His children. "But if anyone seems to be contentious, we do not have such a custom of being so, neither the churches of God" (1 Cor. 11:16). The church in Corinth was apt to strike out on individual lines. All the other churches were going on together with the Lord. It was only Corinth that was out of step; therefore, Paul sought to bring it into line with the others. Today, alas! it is not just one church that has departed from God's way, but the majority of the so-called churches. It is a tragedy that today an injunction to follow "all the churches" would lead, not into, but away from, the will of God!

"Now concerning the collection for the saints, just as I directed the churches of Galatia, so you also do" (1 Cor. 16:1). Paul is saying in effect, "Although you are independent of other churches, yet you must not disregard their example." A willingness to help one another, and to learn from one another, should mark the relationship between the various churches. What the more mature churches have learned from the Lord, the less experienced should be ready to learn from them. "For you, brothers, became imitators of the churches of God which are in Judea in Christ Jesus," wrote Paul to the Thessalonians (1 Thes. 2:14). The church in Thessalonica was younger than the churches in Judea; therefore, it was only fitting that they should learn from them.

There is a beautiful balance in the teaching of God's Word regarding the relationship between the various churches. On the one hand, they are totally independent of one another in matters relating to responsibility, government, and organization. On the other hand, they are to learn from one another and to keep pace with one another. But in everything it is essential to have both the guidance of the Holy Spirit and the pattern in God's Holy Word.

THE HIGHEST COURT

Since there is a spiritual relatedness between the various local churches, no one church may strike out on an individualistic line, and taking advantage of its independence, decide things after its own good pleasure. Each must rather cultivate a relationship with the other churches, seeking their sympathy and working with their spiritual good in view. On the other hand, since each is totally independent of the other, the decision of a church in any locality is absolutely final. There is no higher court of appeal; the local court is the supreme court. There is no organization to whose control it must submit, nor is there any organization over which it exercises control. It has neither superiors nor subordinates. If any one is received or refused by a local church, its judgment in the matter must be regarded as absolutely decisive. Even should the decision be wrong, all that can be done is to appeal for a reconsideration of the case. The local church is the highest church authority. If other churches object to its decisions, all they can do is resort to persuasion and exhortation. There is no alternative course, because the relationship which exists between the churches is purely spiritual, not official.

If a brother who has been disciplined in Nanking moves to Soochow, and there proves himself to be innocent of the charge brought against him, then Soochow has full authority to receive him, despite the judgment of Nanking. Soochow is responsible for its actions to God, not to Nanking. Soochow is an independent church, and has therefore full authority to act as it thinks best. But because there is a spiritual relationship with Nanking, it is well for the brother in question not to be received before Nanking's mistake in judgment is pointed out to Nanking. If Nanking's relationship with the Lord is right, then it will pay attention to what Soochow has to say. But if it refuses to do so, Soochow cannot press anything against Nanking, because Nanking as a local church is directly responsible to the Lord alone, and has full authority to decide and act independently of Soochow. If the churches are spiritual, there will be no difficulty in their relationship one with the other. But if they are not, and difficulties should arise, we must not seek to solve them by interfering in any way with their independence, for it is ordained by an all-wise God.

The organization of no one church is superior to another, nor is its authority greater. Many Christians regard Jerusalem as the mother-church, possessing supreme authority, but such a conception has its source in the human mind, not in the divine Word. Every church is locally governed and is directly responsible to God, not to any other church or organization. A local church is the highest Christian institution on earth. There is none above it to whom appeal can be made. A local church is the lowest scriptural unit, but it is also the highest scriptural organization. Scripture warrants no centralization in Rome which could give Rome authority over other local churches. This is God's safeguard against any infringement of the rights of His Son. Christ is the Head of the Church, and there is no other head in heaven or on earth.

There must be a spiritual relatedness among the churches if the testimony of the Body is to be preserved, but there must at the same time be an absolute independence of government if the testimony of the Head is to be maintained. Each church is under the immediate control of Christ, and is directly responsible to Him alone.

Then why, when a question arose concerning circumcision, did Paul and Barnabas go to Jerusalem to see the apostles and elders there? Because those who were responsible for the erroneous teaching in Antioch had come from Jerusalem. *Jerusalem was the place where this problem originated; therefore, it was to Jerusalem the apostles went to have it settled.* If a boy were caught in mischief, we would report his misdeeds to his father. In going to Jerusalem Paul and Barnabas were bringing the case to those who had control of the brethren who had created trouble, and once they brought the matter to the responsible source, a speedy settlement was effected. The elders in question were not the elders *in* Jerusalem, but the elders *of* Jerusalem; and the apostles were not the apostles *of* Jerusalem, but the apostles *in* Jerusalem. The former were the representatives of the church; the latter, the representatives of the work. Paul and Barnabas referred the matter to the apostles and elders, because the apostles had been responsible for teaching in the churches, and the elders for any decision made regarding local matters. When the apostles and elders both repudiated responsibility concerning the teaching propagated by these troublesome brethren from Jerusalem, Paul and Barnabas on their later visits to different places were able to show to the churches there "the decrees to keep which had been decided upon by the apostles and elders in Jerusalem" (Acts 16:4). We must not infer from this that the elders of Jerusalem had any authority over other churches, but merely that they, as well as the apostles, repudiated the teaching of those who had gone out *from them.* Besides, in Jerusalem some of the apostles occupied the double office of elder and apostle.

HOW TO PRESERVE
THE LOCAL CHARACTER OF THE CHURCHES

Since the churches of God are local, we must be careful to preserve their local character, their local sphere, and their local boundary. Once a church loses these, it ceases to be a scriptural church. Two things call for special attention if the local nature of a church is to be safeguarded.

In the first place, no apostle must exercise control in any official capacity over a church. That is contrary to God's order, and destroys its local nature by putting the imprint of an extra-local minister upon it. No apostle has the authority to establish a private church in any place. The church belongs to the locality, not to the worker. When people are saved by the instrumentality of any man, they belong to the church in the place where they live, not to the man through whom they were saved, nor to the organization he represents. If one or more churches are founded by a certain apostle, and that apostle exercises authority over them as belonging in a special sense to him or to his society, then those churches become sects, for they do not separate themselves from other Christians (saved through the instrumentality of other apostles) on the ground of difference of locality, but on the ground of the difference of instrumentality of salvation. Thus apostles become the heads of different denominations, and their sphere the sphere of their respective denominations, while the churches over which they exercise control become sects, each bearing the particular characteristic of its leader instead of the characteristic of a local church.

The Epistle to the Corinthians throws light on this subject. There was division among the believers in Corinth simply because they failed to realize the local character of the church and sought to make different apostles—Paul, Apollos, and Cephas—the ground of their fellowship. Had they understood the divinely-ordained basis for the division of the Church, they could never have said, "I belong to Paul," or "I belong to Apollos," or "I belong to Cephas," for, despite their especial love for certain leaders, they would have realized that they belonged not to any one of them, but to the church in the locality in which they lived.

No worker may exercise control over a church or attach to it his name or the name of the society he represents. The divine disapproval will always rest on "the church of Paul," or "the church of Apollos," or "the church of Cephas." In the history of the Church it has frequently happened that when God has given special light or experience to any individual, that individual has stressed the particular truth revealed or experienced, and gathered round him people who appreciated his teaching, with the result that the leader, or the truth he emphasized, has become the ground of fellowship. Thus sects have multiplied. If God's people could only see that the object of all ministry is the founding of local churches and not the grouping of Christians around any particular individual, or truth, or experience, or under any particular organization, then the forming of sects would be avoided. We who serve the Lord must be willing to let go our hold upon all those to whom we have ministered, and let all the fruits of our ministry pass into local churches governed entirely by local men. We must be scrupulously careful not to let the coloring of our personality destroy the local character of the church, and we must always serve the church, never control it. An apostle is servant of all and master of none. No church belongs to the worker; it belongs to the locality. Had it been clearly seen by the men who have been used of God throughout the history of the Church that all the churches of God belong to their respective localities, and not to any worker or organization used in their founding, then we should not have so many different denominations today.

Another thing is essential for the preservation of the local character of the church—its sphere must not become wider than the sphere of a locality. The current method of linking up companies of believers in different places who hold the same doctrinal views, and forming them into a church, has no scriptural foundation. The same applies to the custom of regarding any mission as a center, linking together all those saved or helped by them to constitute a "church" of that mission. Such so-called churches are really sects, because they are confined by the bounds of a particular creed, or a particular mission, not by and within the bounds of locality.

The reason God does not sanction the establishing of churches which combine companies of believers in different places is that the divinely-ordained basis for the forming of churches is thereby destroyed. Any "church" formed with a mission as its center is bound to be other than local, because wherever there is a center, there is also a sphere; and if the center of the church is a mission, then obviously its sphere is not the scriptural sphere of locality but the sphere of the mission. It clearly lacks the characteristic of a church, and can only be regarded as a sect. In the purpose of God, Jesus Christ is the *center* of all the churches, and the locality is their sphere.

Whenever a special leader, or a specific doctrine, or some experience, or creed, or organization, becomes a center for drawing together the believers of different places, then because the center of such a church federation is other than Christ, it follows that its sphere will be other than local. And whenever the divinely-appointed sphere of locality is displaced by a sphere of human invention, there the divine approval cannot rest. The believers within such a sphere may truly love the Lord, but they have another center apart from Him, and it is only natural that the second center becomes the controlling one. It is contrary to human nature to stress what we have in common with others; we always emphasize what is ours in particular. Christ is the common center of all the churches, but any company of believers that has a leader, a doctrine, an experience, a creed, or an organization as their center of fellowship, will find that *that* center becomes *the* center, and it is that center by which they determine who belongs to them and who does not. The center always determines the sphere, and the second center creates a sphere which divides those who attach themselves to it from those who do not.

Anything that becomes a center to unite believers of different places will create a sphere which includes all believers who attach themselves to that center and excludes all who do not. This dividing line will destroy the God-appointed boundary of locality, and consequently destroy the very nature of the churches of God. Therefore, the children of God must see to it that they have no center of union apart from Christ, because any extra-local union of believers around a center other than the Lord enlarges the sphere of fellowship beyond the sphere of locality, and thus the specific characteristic of the churches of God is lost. *There are no other churches in Scripture but local churches!*

THE BENEFITS OF INDEPENDENCE

The divine method of making locality the boundary line between the different churches has various obvious advantages:

(1) If each church is locally governed, and all authority is in the hands of the local elders, there is no scope for an able and ambitious false prophet to display his organizing genius

by forming the different companies of believers into one vast federation, and then satisfy his ambition by constituting himself its head. Rome could never sway the power it does today had the churches of God maintained their local ground. Where churches are not affiliated, and where local authority is in the hands of local elders, a pope is an impossibility. Where there are only local churches, there can be no Roman Church. It is the federation of different companies of believers that has brought such evils as dabbling in politics into the Church of God. There is power in a federated "church," but it is carnal power, not spiritual. God's thought for His Church is that she should be like a mustard seed on earth, full of vitality, yet scarcely noticed. It is federation that has brought the Church of today to the state of Thyatira. The failure of Protestantism is that it has substituted organized churches— State and Dissenting—for the Church of Rome, instead of returning to the divinely-ordained local churches.

(2) Further, if the churches retain their local character, the spread of heresy and error will be avoided, for if a church is local, heresy and error will be local too. Rome is a splendid illustration of the reverse side of this truth. The prevalence of Romish error is because of Romish federation. The sphere of the federated churches is vast; consequently the error is widespread. It is a comparatively simple matter to quarantine error in a local church, but to isolate error in a vast federation of churches is quite another proposition.

(3) The greatest advantage of having locality as the boundary of the churches is that it precludes all possibility of sects. You may have your special doctrines and I mine, but as long as we are out to maintain the scriptural character of the churches by making locality the only dividing line between them, then it is impossible for us to establish any church for the propagation of our particular beliefs. As long as a church preserves its local character, it is protected against denominationalism, but as soon as it loses that, it is veering in the direction of sectarianism. A believer is sectarian when he belongs to anyone or anything apart from the Lord and the locality. Sects and denominations can only be established when the local character of the church is destroyed.

In the wisdom of God He has decreed that all His churches be local. This is the divine method of safeguarding them against sects. Obviously, it can only protect the Church against sectarianism in expression. It is still possible for a sectarian spirit to exist in a non-sectarian church, and only the Spirit of God can deal with that. May we all learn to walk after the Spirit and not after the flesh, so that both in outward expression and inward condition the churches of God may be well-pleasing to Him.

CHAPTER FIVE

THE BASIS OF UNION AND DIVISION

THE FORMING OF LOCAL CHURCHES

In the previous chapter we observed that the word "church" was only mentioned twice in the Gospels. It is used frequently in the Acts, but we are never explicitly told there how a church was formed. The second chapter speaks of the salvation of about three thousand men, and the fourth chapter of a further five thousand, but nothing whatever is said about these believers forming a church. Without a single word of explanation they are referred to in the following chapter as the church—"And great fear came upon the whole church" (5:11). Here the Scriptures call the children of God "the church," without even mentioning how the church came into being. In Acts 8:1, immediately after the death of Stephen, the word is again used, and the connection in this case is clearer than before. "There occurred in that day a great persecution against the church which was in Jerusalem." From this passage it is obvious that the believers in Jerusalem are the church in Jerusalem. So we know now what the church is. It consists of all the saved ones in a given locality.

Later on, in the course of the apostles' first missionary tour, many people were saved in different places through the preaching of the gospel. Nothing is mentioned about their being formed into churches, but in Acts 14:23, it is said of Paul and Barnabas that "they had appointed elders for them in every church." The groups of believers in these different places are called churches, without any explanation whatever as to how they came to be churches. They *were* groups of believers, so they simply *were* churches. Whenever a number of people in any place were saved, they spontaneously became the church in that place. Without introduction or explanation of any kind, the Word of God presents such a group of believers to us as a church. The scriptural method of founding a church is simply by preaching the gospel; nothing further is necessary, or even permissible. If people hear the gospel and receive the Lord as their Savior, then they *are* a church; there is no need of any further procedure in order to *become* a church.

If in a given place anyone believes on the Lord, as a matter of course he is a constituent of the church in that place; there is no further step necessary in order to make him a constituent. No subsequent joining is required of him. Provided he belongs to the Lord, he already belongs to the church in that locality; and since he *already* belongs to the church, his belonging cannot be made subject to any condition. If, before recognizing a believer as a member of the church, we insist that he join us, or that he resign his connection elsewhere, then "our church" is decidedly not one of the churches of God. If we impose any conditions of membership upon a believer in the locality, we are immediately in an unscriptural position, because his being a member of the local church is conditioned only by his being a believer in the locality. All the saved ones who belong to the place in which we live belong to the same church as we do. I mean by the church a scriptural church, and not a man-made organization. *A local church is a church which comprises all the children of God in a given locality.*

Let us note well that the ground of our receiving anyone into the church is that the Lord has already received that one. "Him who is weak in faith receive...for God has received him" (Rom. 14:1, 3). "Therefore receive one another, as Christ also received you" (15:7). Our receiving anyone is merely our recognition that the Lord has already received him. Our receiving him does not make him a member of the church; rather, it is that we receive him because he is already a member. If he is the Lord's, he is in the church. If he is not the Lord's, he is not in the church. If we demand anything beyond his reception by the Lord before admitting him to fellowship, then we are not a church at all, but only a sect.

WITHIN AND WITHOUT THE CIRCLE

In any place where the gospel has been proclaimed and people have believed on the Lord, they are the church in that place, and they are our brethren. In the days of the apostles the question of belonging or not belonging to a church was simple in the extreme. But things are not so simple in our days, for the question has been complicated by many so-called churches that exclude those who should be in the church, and include those who should be outside. What sort of a person can be rightly considered a constituent of the church? What is the minimum requirement we can insist upon for admission to church fellowship? Unless the qualifications for church membership are clearly defined, there will always be the danger of excluding from the church those who truly belong to it and including those who do not.

Before we proceed to discover who really belongs to a local church and who does not, let us first inquire who belongs to the universal Church and who does not, since the condition of membership in a church is essentially the same as in the Church. When we know what kind of persons belong to the Church, then we know also what kind of persons belong to a church.

How can we know who is a Christian and who is not? "If anyone does not have the Spirit of Christ, he is not of Him" (Rom. 8:9). According to the Word of God, every person in whose heart Christ dwells by His Spirit is a true Christian. Christians may differ from one another in a thousand respects, but in this fundamental matter there is no difference between them: one and all have the Spirit of Christ dwelling within them. If we wish to know who belongs to the Lord, then we only need to discover whether he has the Spirit of Christ or not. Whoever has the Spirit of Christ is inside the Church circle, and whoever does not have the Spirit of Christ is outside the circle. A participant of the Spirit of God is an essential part of the Church of God; a non-participant of the Spirit of God has no part in the Church. In the Church universal this is true; in the church local this is also true. "Test yourselves whether you are in the faith; prove yourselves. Or do you not realize about yourselves that Jesus Christ is in you, unless you are disapproved?" (2 Cor. 13:5). There is a subjective line of demarcation between the Church and the world; all within that line are saved, and all without that line are lost. This line of demarcation is the indwelling Spirit of Christ.

THE ONENESS OF THE SPIRIT

The Church of God includes a vast number of believers, living at different times, and scattered in different places throughout the earth. How has it come about that all have been united into *one* universal Church? With such differences in age, social position, education, background, outlook, and temperament, how could all these people become one church? What is the secret of the oneness of the saints? By what means has Christianity caused these people, with their thousand differences, to become truly one? It is not that, having a grand convention and agreeing to be one, Christians become united. Christian unity is no human product; its origin is purely divine. This mighty mysterious oneness is planted in the hearts of all believers the moment they receive the Lord. It is "the oneness of the Spirit" (Eph. 4:3).

The Spirit who dwells in the heart of every believer is one Spirit; therefore, He makes all those in whom He dwells to be one, even as He Himself is one. Christians may differ from one another in innumerable ways, but all Christians of all ages, with their countless differences, have this one fundamental likeness—the Spirit of God dwells in every one of them. *This is the secret of the oneness of believers, and this is the secret of their separation from the world.* The reason for Christian unity and for Christian separation is one.

It is this inherent unity that makes all believers one, and it is this inherent unity that accounts for the impossibility of division between believers, except for geographical reasons. Those who do not have this are outsiders; those who have it are our brethren. If you have the Spirit of Christ and I have the Spirit of Christ, then we both belong to the same Church. There is no need to *be* united; we *are* united by the one Spirit who dwells in us both. Paul besought all believers to endeavor "to keep the oneness of the Spirit" (Eph. 4:3); he did not exhort us to have the oneness, but merely to keep it. We have it already, for obviously we cannot keep what we do not have. God has never told us to become one with other believers; we already *are* one. Therefore, we do not need to create oneness; we only need to maintain it.

We cannot *make* this oneness, since by the Spirit we *are* one in Christ, and we cannot *break* it, because it is an eternal fact in Christ; but we can destroy *the effects* of it, so that its expression in the Church is lost. Alas! that we have not only failed to preserve this precious oneness, but have actually so destroyed the fruits of it, that there is little outward trace of oneness among the children of God.

How are we going to determine who are our brothers and our fellow members in the Church of God? Not by inquiring if they hold the same doctrinal views that we hold, or have had the same spiritual experiences; nor by seeing if their customs, manner of living, interests, and preferences tally with ours. We merely inquire, Are they indwelt by the Spirit of God or not? We cannot insist on oneness of opinions, or oneness of experience, or any other oneness among believers, except the oneness of the Spirit. That oneness there can be, and always must be, among the children of God. All who have this oneness are in the Church.

In your travels has it not sometimes happened that on a boat or train you have met a stranger, and after only a few moments of conversation you have found a pure love for him welling up in your heart? That spontaneous outgoing of love was because of the one Spirit dwelling in both hearts. Such inner spiritual oneness transcends all social, racial, and national differences.

How can we know whether or not a person has this oneness of the Spirit? In the verse immediately following Paul's exhortation to keep the oneness of the Spirit, he explains what those have in common who possess this oneness. We cannot expect believers to be alike in everything, but there are seven things which all true believers share, and by the existence or absence of these we can know whether or not a person has the oneness of the Spirit. Many other things are of great importance, but these seven are vital. They are indispensable to spiritual fellowship, and they are at once the minimum and the maximum requirements that can be made of any person who professes to be a fellow believer.

SEVEN FACTORS IN SPIRITUAL ONENESS

"One Body and one Spirit, even as also you were called in one hope of your calling; one Lord, one faith, one baptism; one God and Father of all, who is over all and through all and in all" (Eph. 4:4-6). A person is constituted a member of the Church on the ground that he possesses the oneness of the Spirit, and that will result in his being one with all believers on the above seven points. They are the seven elements in the oneness of the Spirit, which is the common heritage of all the children of God. In drawing a line of demarcation between those who belong to the Church and those who do not, we must require nothing beyond these seven lest we exclude any who belong to the family of God; and we dare not require anything less, lest we include any who do not belong to the divine family. All in whom these seven are found belong to the Church; all who lack any of them do not belong to the Church.

(1) ONE BODY. The question of oneness begins with the question of membership of the Body of Christ. The sphere of our fellowship is the sphere of the Body. Those who are outside that sphere have no spiritual relationship with us, but those who are inside that sphere are all in fellowship with us. We cannot make any choice of fellowship in the Body, accepting some members and rejecting others. We are all part of the one Body, and nothing can possibly separate us from it, or from one another. Anyone who has received Christ belongs to the Body, and he and we are one. If we do not wish to extend fellowship to anyone, we must first make sure that he does not belong to the Body; if he does, we have no reason to reject him (unless for such disciplinary reasons as are clearly laid down in the Word of God).

(2) ONE SPIRIT. If anyone seeks fellowship with us, however he may differ from us in experience or outlook, provided he has the same Spirit as we have, he is entitled

THE BASIS OF UNION AND DIVISION 79

to be received as a brother. If he has received the Spirit of Christ, and we have received the Spirit of Christ, then we are one in the Lord, and nothing must divide us.

(3) ONE HOPE. This hope, which is common to all the children of God, is not a general hope, but the hope of our calling, that is, the hope of our calling as Christians. What is our hope as Christians? We hope to be with the Lord forever in glory. There is not a single soul who is truly the Lord's in whose heart there is not this hope, for to have Christ in us is to have "the hope of glory" in us (Col. 1:27). If anyone claims to be the Lord's, but has no hope of heaven or glory, his is a mere empty profession. All who share this one hope are one, and since we have the hope of being together in glory for all eternity, how can we be divided in time? If we are going to share the same future, shall we not gladly share the same present?

(4) ONE LORD. There is only one Lord, the Lord Jesus, and all who recognize that God has made Jesus of Nazareth to be both Lord and Christ are one in Him. If anyone confesses Jesus to be Lord, then his Lord is our Lord, and since we serve the same Lord, nothing whatever can separate us.

(5) ONE FAITH. The faith here spoken of is *the* faith—not our beliefs in regard to the interpretation of Scripture, but the faith through which we have been saved, which is the common possession of all believers; that is, the faith that Jesus is the Son of God (who died for the salvation of sinners and lives again to give life to the dead). Anyone who lacks this vital faith does not belong to the Lord, but all who possess it are the Lord's. The children of God may follow many different lines of scriptural interpretation, but in regard to this fundamental faith they are one. Those who lack this faith have no part in the family of God, but all who possess it we recognize as our brothers in the Lord.

(6) ONE BAPTISM. Is it by immersion or by sprinkling? Is it single or triune? There are various forms of baptism accepted by the children of God, so if we make the form of baptism the dividing line between those who belong to the church and those who do not, we shall exclude many true believers from our fellowship. There are children of God who

even believe that a material baptism is not necessary, but since they *are* the children of God, we dare not on that account exclude them from our fellowship. What then is the significance of the one baptism mentioned in this passage? Paul throws light on the subject in his first letter to the Corinthians. "Is Christ divided? Was Paul crucified for you? Or were you baptized into the name of Paul?" (1:13). The emphasis is not on the form of baptism, but on the *name* into which we are baptized. The first question is not whether you are sprinkled or immersed, dipped once or three times, baptized literally or spiritually; the important point is this: Into *whose name* have you been baptized? If you are baptized into the name of the Lord, that is your qualification for church membership. If anyone is baptized into the name of the Lord, I welcome him as my brother, whatever the manner of his baptism. *By this we do not imply that it is of no consequence whether we are sprinkled or immersed, or whether our baptism is spiritual or literal. The Word of God teaches that baptism is literal, and is by immersion,* but the point here is that the manner of baptism is not the ground of our fellowship, but the name into which we are baptized. All who are baptized into the name of the Lord are one in Him.

(7) ONE GOD. Do we believe in the same personal, supernatural God as our Father? If so, then we belong to one family, and there is no adequate reason for our being divided.

The above seven points are the seven factors in that divine oneness which is the possession of all the members of the divine family, and they constitute the only test of Christian profession. They are the possession of every true Christian, no matter to what place or period he belongs. Like a sevenfold cord the oneness of the Spirit binds all the believers throughout the world; and however diverse their character or circumstances, provided they have these seven expressions of an inner oneness, then nothing can possibly separate them.

If we impose any conditions of fellowship beyond these seven—which are but the outcome of the one spiritual life, then we are guilty of sectarianism, for we are making a division between those who are manifestly children of God. If we apply any test but these seven, such as baptism by immersion, or certain interpretations of prophecy, or a special line of holiness teaching, or a so-called Pentecostal experience, or the resigning from any denominational church—then we are imposing conditions other than those stipulated in the Word of God. All who have these seven points in common with us are our brothers, whatever their spiritual experience, or doctrinal views, or so-called church relationships. Our oneness is not based on our appreciation of the truth of our oneness, nor on our coming out from all that would contradict our oneness, but upon the *actual fact* of our oneness, which is made real in our experience by the indwelling Spirit of Christ.

LOCAL CHURCHES

Now what is true of the universal Church is also true of a local church. The universal Church comprises all those who have the oneness of the Spirit. The local church comprises all those who, in a given locality, have the oneness of the Spirit. The Church of God and the churches of God do not differ in nature, but only in extent. The former consists of all throughout the universe who are indwelt by the Spirit of God; the latter consists of all in one locality who are indwelt by the Spirit.

Anyone wishing to belong to a church in a given locality must answer two requirements—he must be a child of God, and he must live in that particular locality. Membership in *the Church of God* is conditioned only by being a child of God, but membership in a *church of God* is conditioned, firstly, by being a child of God and, secondly, by living in a given locality.

In nature the Church is indivisible as God Himself is indivisible. Therefore, the division of the Church into churches is not a division in nature, life, or essence, but only in government, organization, and management. Because the earthly church is composed of a vast number of individuals, a measure of organization is indispensable. It is a physical impossibility for all the people of God, scattered throughout the world, to live and meet in one place; and it is for that reason alone that the Church of God has been divided into churches.

We must realize clearly that the nature of all the local churches is the same throughout the whole earth. It is not that the constituents of one local church are of one kind, and the constituents of another local church are of another kind. In nature there is no difference whatever. The only difference is in the localities that determine their respective boundaries. The Church is indivisible; therefore, in nature the churches are indivisible too. It is only in outward sphere that there is any possibility of dividing them. Physical limitations make geographical divisions inevitable, but the spiritual oneness of believers overcomes all barriers of space.

Locality is the divinely-appointed ground for the division of the Church, because it is the only inevitable division. Every barrier between all believers in the world is avoidable, except this one. As long as believers remain in the flesh they cannot exist apart from their dwelling places; therefore, the churches which consist of such believers cannot but be restricted by their dwellings. Geographical distinctions are natural, not arbitrary, and it is simply because the physical limitations of the children of God make geographical divisions inevitable, that God has ordained that His Church be divided into churches on the ground of locality. Such division is scriptural, and all other divisions are carnal. *Any division of the children of God other than geographical implies not merely a division of sphere, but a division of nature. Local division is the only division which does not touch the life of the Church.*

Most believers of today are so utterly blind to the scriptural basis of a church that if one asks another, "To what church do you belong?" The first thought of the one questioned is of the specific line of teaching he approves of, or the group of people with whom he has special fellowship, or how his group of Christians is different from others, or perhaps the name that particular group bears, or the form of organization they have adopted—in short, *anything but the place* in which he lives. Few would answer that question with, "I belong to the church in Ephesus," or "I belong to the church in Shanghai," or "I belong to the church in Los Angeles." It is our being in Christ that separates us from the world, and it is our being in a given locality that separates us from other believers. It is only because we reside in a different place from them that we belong to a different church. The only reason I do not belong to the same church as other believers is that I do not live in the same place as they do. If I wish to be in the same church, then I must change my residence to the same place. If, on the other hand, I wish to be in a different church from others in my locality, then the only solution to my problem is to move to a different locality. Difference of locality is the only justification for division among believers.

SEVEN FORBIDDEN GROUNDS OF DIVISION

On the positive side we have just seen the ground on which God has ordained that His Church be divided. Now, on the negative side, we shall see on what ground the Church ought not to be divided.

(1) SPIRITUAL LEADERS. "Now I mean this, that each of you says, I am of Paul, and I of Apollos, and I of Cephas, and I of Christ" (1 Cor. 1:12). Here Paul points out the carnality of the Corinthian believers in attempting to divide the church of God in Corinth, which, by the divine ordering, was indivisible, being already the smallest scriptural unit upon which any church could be established. They sought to divide the church on the ground of a few leaders who had been specially used of God in their midst. Cephas was a zealous minister of the gospel, Paul was a man who had suffered much for his Lord's sake, and Apollos was one whom God certainly used in His service, but though all three had been indisputably owned of God in Corinth, God could never permit the church there to make them a ground of division. He ordained that His Church be divided on the basis of localities, not of persons. It was all right to have a church in Corinth and a church in Ephesus, and quite all right to have several churches in Galatia and a number in Macedonia, for difference of locality justified division into these various churches. It was also all right for the believers to esteem those leaders whom God had used among them, but it would have been quite wrong to divide the churches according to the respective leaders by whom they had been helped.

Paul, Cephas, and Apollos were true-hearted servants of God who allowed no party-spirit to separate them; it was their followers who were responsible for the separation. Hero worship is a tendency of human nature, which delights to show preference for those who appeal to its tastes. Because so many of God's children know little or nothing of the power of the cross to deal with the flesh, this tendency to worship a man has expressed itself frequently in the Church of God, and much havoc has been wrought in consequence. It is in keeping with God's will that we should learn from spiritual men and profit by their leadership, but it is altogether contrary to His will that we should divide the Church according to the men we admire. *The only scriptural basis for the forming of a church is difference of locality, not difference of leaders.*

(2) INSTRUMENTS OF SALVATION. Spiritual leaders are no adequate reason for dividing the Church; neither are the instruments used of God in our salvation. Some of the Corinthian believers proclaimed themselves to be "of Cephas," others "of Paul," others "of Apollos." They traced the beginning of their spiritual history to these men, and so thought they belonged to them. It is both natural and common for persons saved through the instrumentality of a worker, or a society, to consider themselves as belonging to such a worker or society. It is likewise both natural and common for an individual, or a mission, through whose means people have been saved, to consider the saved ones as belonging to them. It is natural, but not spiritual. It is common, but nevertheless, contrary to God's will. Alas! that so many of God's servants have not yet realized that they are servants of the local church, not masters of a private "church." *Churches are divided on the ground of geography, not on the ground of the instruments of our salvation.*

(3) NON-SECTARIANISM. Some Christians think they know better than to say, "I am of Cephas," or "I am of Paul," or "I am of Apollos." They say, "I am of Christ." Such Christians despise the others as sectarian, and on that ground start another community. Their attitude is—"*You* are sectarian; I

am non-sectarian. *You* are hero worshippers; *we* worship the Lord alone."

But God's Word condemns not only those who say, "I am of Cephas," "I am of Paul," or "I am of Apollos." It just as definitely and just as clearly denounces those who say, "I am of Christ." It is not wrong to consider oneself as belonging only to Christ; it is right and even essential. Nor is it wrong to repudiate all schism among the children of God; it is highly commendable. God does not condemn this class of Christians for either of these two things; He condemns them for the very sin they condemn in others—their sectarianism. As a protest against division among the children of God, many believers seek to divide those who do not divide from those who do, and never dream that they themselves are divisive! Their ground of division may be more plausible than that of others who divide on the ground of doctrinal differences, or personal preference for certain leaders, but the fact remains that they *are* dividing the children of God. Even while they repudiate schism elsewhere, they are schismatic themselves.

When you say, "I am of Christ," do you mean to say others are not? It is perfectly legitimate for you to say, "I am of Christ," if your remark merely implies to whom you belong; but if it implies, "I am not sectarian; I stand quite differently from you sectarians," then it is making a difference between you and other Christians. The very thought of *distinguishing* between the children of God has its springs in the carnal nature of man, and is sectarian. If we look on other believers as sectarian and consider ourselves to be non-sectarian, we are immediately differentiating between God's people and thereby manifesting a divisive spirit even in the very act of condemning division. No matter by what means we distinguish between the members of God's family—even if it be on the pretext of Christ Himself—we are guilty of schism in the Body.

What then is right? All exclusiveness is wrong. All inclusiveness (of true children of God) is right. Denominations are not scriptural, and we ought to have no part in them, but if we adopt an attitude of criticism and think, "*They* are denominational; I am undenominational. *They* belong to sects;

I belong to Christ alone"—such differentiating is definitely sectarian.

Yes, praise God I *am* of Christ, but my fellowship is not merely with those who *say,* "I am of Christ," but with all who *are* of Christ. What is of vital importance is not the confession, but the fact. Although these other believers *say* they are of Paul, of Cephas, and of Apollos, yet *in fact* they are of Christ. I do not so much mind what they *say,* but I very much mind what they *are.* I do not inquire whether they are denominational or undenominational, sectarian or unsectarian; I only inquire, "Are they of Christ?" If they are of Christ, then they are my brethren.

Our personal standing should be undenominational, but the basis of our fellowship is not undenominationalism. *We ourselves should be non-sectarian, but we dare not insist on non-sectarianism as a condition of fellowship. Our only ground of fellowship is Christ.* Our fellowship must be with *all the believers* in a locality, not merely with *all the unsectarian believers* in that locality. *They* may make denominational differences, but *we* must not make undenominational requirements. We dare not differentiate between ourselves and them, because they differentiate between themselves and others. They are the children of God, and because they make distinctions between themselves and other children of God, they do not on that account cease to be the children of God. Their denominationalism or sectarianism will mean that severe limitations are imposed upon the Lord as to His purpose and mind for them, and this will mean that they will never go beyond a certain measure of spiritual growth and fullness. Blessing there may be, but fullness of divine purpose never.

All believers living in the same locality belong to the same church. This is an unchanging principle. We dare not alter "all the believers in a locality" to "all the undenominational believers in a locality." If we make undenominationalism or unsectarianism the boundary of our church, instead of locality, then we lose our local standing as a church and become a sect. It is not a denominational church, nor an interdenominational church, nor even an undenominational church we are after, but a *local* church. The difference between a local church and an undenominational church is as vast as the difference between heaven and earth. A local church is undenominational, but an undenominational church is denominational. "The church in Corinth" is scriptural, but "the church of all those who say, 'I am of Christ' in Corinth" is unscriptural. Our work is positive and constructive, not negative and destructive. We are out to establish churches, not to destroy denominations. Human nature is prone to go to extremes; it is so easy for us either to be undenominational ourselves and demand undenominationalism of others, or else to tolerate denominationalism in others and gradually become denominational ourselves. We ourselves *must* be undenominational, but we must not demand undenominationalism of other Christians as the basis of our fellowship.

Therefore, if we come to a place where Christ is not named, we must preach the gospel, win men to the Lord, and found a local church. If we come to a place where there are already Christians, but on various grounds these believers separate themselves into denominational "churches," our task is just the same as in the other place—we must preach the gospel, lead men to the Lord, and form them into a church on the scriptural ground of locality. All the while we must maintain an attitude of inclusiveness, not exclusiveness, towards those believers who are in different sects, for they, as we, are children of God, and they live in the same locality; therefore, they belong to the same church as we do. For ourselves, we cannot join any sect or remain in one, for our church connection can only be on local ground, but in regard to others we must not make leaving a sect the condition of fellowship with those believers who are in a sect. That will make undenominationalism our church ground, instead of locality. Let us be clear on this point, that an undenominational church is not a local church. There is a vast difference between the two. A local church is undenominational, and it is positive and inclusive; but an undenominational church is not a local church, and it is negative and exclusive.

Let us be clear as to our position. We are not out to establish undenominational churches, but local churches. We are seeking to do a positive work. If believers can be led to see what a local church is—the expression of the Body of Christ in a locality—they will certainly not remain in any sect. On the other hand, it is possible for them to see all the evils of sectarianism, and leave them, without knowing what a local church is. We must help those, to whom God has been pleased to use us, to understand clearly the truth regarding local churches, and not to lay emphasis on the question of denominations. They must realize that whenever they use the term "we" in relation to the children of God, they must include all the children of God, not merely those who are meeting with them. If when we say "our brethren," we do not include all the children of God, but only those who continually meet with us, then we are schismatic.

I do not condone sectarianism, and I do not believe we should belong to any sect, but it is not our business to get people to leave them. If we make it our chief concern to lead people to a real knowledge of the Lord and the power of His cross, then they will gladly abandon themselves to Him, and will learn to walk in the Spirit, repudiating the things of the flesh. We shall find there will be no need to stress the question of denominations, for the Spirit Himself will enlighten them. If a believer has not learned the way of the cross and the walk in the Spirit, what is gained by his coming out of a sect?

(4) DOCTRINAL DIFFERENCES. In the Greek the word rendered "heresies" in Galatians 5:20 [KJV] does not necessarily convey the thought of error, but rather of division on the ground of doctrine. The Interlinear New Testament translates it as "sects," while Darby in his New Translation renders it "schools of opinion." The whole thought here is not of the difference between truth and error, but of division based upon doctrine. My teaching may be right or it may be wrong, but if I make it a cause of division, then I am guilty of the "heresy" spoken of here.

God forbids any division on doctrinal grounds. Some believe that rapture is pre-tribulation; others, that it is post-tribulation. Some believe that all the saints will enter the kingdom; others believe that only a section will enter. Some believe that baptism is by immersion; others, that is by sprinkling. Some believe that supernatural manifestations are a necessary accompaniment to the baptism in the Holy Spirit, while others do not. None of these doctrinal views constitute a scriptural basis for separating the children of God. Though some may be right and others wrong, God does not sanction any division on account of difference as to such beliefs.[1] If a group of believers split off from a local church in their zeal for certain teaching according to the Word of God, the new "church" they establish may have more scriptural teaching, but it could never be a scriptural church. To bring error into a church is carnal, but to divide a church on account of error may also be carnal. It is carnality that so often destroys the oneness of the church in any place.

If we wish to maintain a scriptural position, then we must see to it that the churches we found in various places *only represent localities, not doctrines.* If our "church" is not separated from other children of God on the ground of locality alone, but stands for the propagation of some particular doctrine, then we are decidedly a sect, however true to the Word of God our teaching may be. The purpose of God is that a church should represent the children of God in a locality, not represent some specific truth there. *A church of God in any place comprises all the children of God in that place, not merely those who hold the same doctrinal views.*

Should we arrive at a place where a church has already been established on clear local ground, and discover that its members hold views which we consider unscriptural, or that they consider the views we hold as unscriptural, if we then refuse to recognize them as the church of God in that locality and withdraw from fellowship, we are divisive. The question is not whether they agree with our presentation of truth, but whether they are standing on clear church ground.

If our hearts are set to preserve the local character of the churches of God, we cannot fail to come up against problems

---

[1] We are not, of course, dealing here with the foundations of the faith, the essential doctrines of the divine Persons, faith in Christ, atonement, etc., but subsequent matters.

in our work. Unless the cross operates mightily, what endless possibilities of friction there will be if we include in one church all the believers in the locality with all their varying views. How the flesh would like just to include those holding the same views, and to exclude all whose views differ from ours. To have constant and close association with people whose interpretation of Scripture does not tally with ours, is hard for the flesh, but good for the spirit. God does not use division to solve the problem; He uses the cross. He would have us submit to the cross, so that through the very difficulties of the situation, the meekness and patience and love of Christ may be deeply wrought into our lives. Under the circumstances, if we do not know the cross, we shall probably argue, lose our temper, and finally go our own way. We may have right views, but God is giving us an opportunity to display a right attitude; we may believe aright, but God is testing us to see if we love aright. It is easy to have a mind well stored with scriptural teaching, and a heart devoid of true love. Those who differ from us will be a means in God's hand to test whether we have spiritual experience, or only scriptural knowledge, to test whether the truths we proclaim are a matter of life to us, or mere theory.

Romans 14 shows us how to deal with those whose views differ from ours. What would we do if in our church there were vegetarians and Sabbatarians? Why, we should consider it almost intolerable if in the same church some of the believers kept the Lord's Day and others the Sabbath, and some ate meat freely, while others were strict vegetarians. That was exactly the situation Paul was facing. Let us note his conclusions. "Now him who is weak in faith receive, but not for the purpose of passing judgment on his considerations" (v. 1). "Who are you who judge another's household servant? To his own master he stands or falls; and he will be made to stand, for the Lord is able to make him stand" (v. 4). "Therefore let us judge one another no longer, but rather judge this: not to put a stumbling block or cause of falling before your brother" (v. 13) Oh, for Christian tolerance! Oh, for largeness of heart! Alas! that many of God's children are so zealous for their pet doctrines that they immediately label

THE BASIS OF UNION AND DIVISION

as heretics, and treat accordingly, all whose interpretation of Scripture differs from theirs. God would have us walk in love toward all who hold views contrary to those views that are dear to us (v. 15).

This does not mean that all the members of a church can hold whatever views they please, but it does mean that the solution to the problem of doctrinal differences does not lie in forming separate parties according to the different views held, but in walking in love toward those whose outlook differs from ours. By patient teaching we may yet be able to help all to "the oneness of the faith" (Eph. 4:13). As we wait patiently on the Lord, He may grant grace to the others to change their views, or He may grant us grace to see that we are not such good teachers as we thought we were. Nothing so tests the spirituality of a teacher as opposition to his teaching.

The teachers must learn humility, but so must all the other believers. When they recognize their position in the Body, they will know that it is not given to everyone to determine matters of doctrine. They must learn to submit to those who have been equipped of God for the specific ministry of teaching His people. Spiritual gifts and spiritual experience are necessary for spiritual teaching; consequently not everyone can teach.

"Make my joy full, that you think the same thing, having the same love, joined in soul, thinking the one thing, doing nothing by way of selfish ambition nor by way of vainglory, but in lowliness of mind considering one another more excellent than yourselves; not regarding each his own virtues, but each the virtues of others also" (Phil. 2:2-4). When the churches have laid to heart what Paul wrote to the church in Philippi, then it will be perfectly possible to have only one church in one locality with no friction whatever among its many members.

(5) RACIAL DIFFERENCES. "For also in one Spirit we were all baptized into one body, whether Jews or Greeks, whether slaves or free, and were all given to drink one Spirit" (1 Cor. 12:13). Jews have always had the strongest racial prejudice of all peoples. They regarded other nations as unclean, and were forbidden even to eat with them; but Paul made it very

clear, in writing to the Corinthians, that in the Church both Jew and Gentile are one. All distinctions in Adam have been done away with in Christ. A racial *"church"* has no recognition in the Word of God. Church membership is determined by place of residence, not by race.

Today in the large cosmopolitan cities of the world there are churches for the whites and churches for the blacks, churches for the Europeans and churches for the Asiatics. These have originated through failure to understand that the boundary of a church is a city. God does not permit any division of His children on the ground of difference of color, custom, or manner of living. No matter to what race they belong, if they belong to the same locality, they belong to the same church. God has placed believers of different races in one locality, so that, by transcending all external differences, they might in one church show forth the one life and the one Spirit of His Son. All that comes to us by nature is overcome by grace. All that was ours in Adam has been ruled out in Christ. The whole matter hinges here—are all carnal differences done away with in Christ, or is there still a place for the flesh in the Church? Are our resources in Christ sufficient to overcome all natural barriers? Let us remember that the church in any locality includes all the believers living there and excludes all who live elsewhere.

(6) NATIONAL DIFFERENCES. Jews and Gentiles represent national as well as racial distinctions, but in the Church of God there is neither Jew nor Greek. There is no racial distinction there, and there is no national distinction either. All believers living in one place, no matter what their nationality, belong to the one church. In the natural realm there is a difference between Chinese, French, British, and Americans, but in the spiritual realm there is none. If a Chinese believer lives in Nanking, he belongs to the church in Nanking. If a French believer lives in Nanking, he also belongs to the church in Nanking. The same holds good for Britishers, Americans, and all other nationalities, provided they are born again. The Word of God recognizes the church in Rome, the church in Ephesus, and the church in Thessalonica, but it does not recognize the Jewish church, or the

THE BASIS OF UNION AND DIVISION 93

Chinese church, or the Anglican church. The reason the names of cities appear in Scripture in connection with the churches of God is that the difference of dwelling place is the only difference recognized by God among His children. Their life is essentially one, and is therefore indivisible, but the place in which that life is lived cannot but vary as long as they remain in the flesh.

Since the churches are all local, if a believer—whatever his nationality—moves from one place to another, he immediately becomes a member of the church in the latter place, and has no church connection in the place of his former residence. You cannot live in one place and be a member of the church in another. There is no extraterritoriality in connection with the churches of God. As soon as you exceed the city limit, you exceed the church limit. If a Chinese brother moves from Nanking to Hankow, he becomes a member of the church in Hankow. In like manner, a British brother coming from London to Hankow immediately becomes a member of the church in Hankow. A change of residence necessarily involves a change of church, whereas naturalization has no effect on church membership.

Our fellow workers who have gone from China to the South Sea Islands must be careful not to form an Overseas Chinese church there. It is possible to have an Overseas Chinese Chamber of Commerce, or an Overseas Chinese College, or an Overseas Chinese Club. Anything you like can be Overseas Chinese, but not a church. A church is always local! If you go to any city in a foreign land, then it follows as a matter of course that you belong to the church in that city. There is nothing Chinese about the churches of God.

How glorious it would be if the saved in every city could overlook all natural differences and only consider their spiritual oneness. "We are the believers in Christ in such-and-such a place" is the finest confession a company of Christians can make. Whether Christ is in you or not, determines whether or not you belong to the Church; where you live determines the particular church to which you belong. The question put by God to the world is, "Do they belong to Christ?" The question put by God to believers is, "Where do they live?" Not nationality but locality is the question raised. *The churches of God are built on city ground, not on national ground.*

The usual conception of an indigenous church, while quite right in some respects, is fundamentally wrong at the most vital point. Since the divine method of dividing the Church is according to locality, not nationality, then all differentiation between Christian and heathen countries is contrary to God's thought. The Church of God knows neither Jew nor Greek; therefore, it knows neither native nor foreigner, neither heathen country nor Christian country. The Scriptures differentiate between cities, not between countries, heathen and Christian. So if we would be in full accord with the mind of God, we must make no difference whatever between the Chinese and foreign church, between Chinese and foreign workers, or between Chinese and foreign funds.

The thought of the indigenous church is that the natives of a country should be self-governing, self-supporting, and self-propagating, while the thought of God is that the believers *in a city—whether native or foreign—should be self-governing, self-supporting, and self-propagating.* Take, for instance, Peking. The theory of the indigenous church distinguishes between Chinese and foreigners in Peking, whereas the Word of God distinguishes between the believers in Peking—whether Chinese or foreign—and the believers in other cities. That is why in Scripture we read of the churches of the Gentiles, but never of the church of the Gentiles. The attempt to form all Chinese believers into one church shows a lack of understanding in regard to the divine basis of forming churches.

On the one hand, there is no church of the Gentiles in Scripture; on the other hand, we read of "the church of the Thessalon*ians*." It is suggestive that this is the only expression of its kind used in the New Testament. The Word does not speak of the church of the Greeks (a race, or nation), but of the church of the Thessalonians (a city). There is no such thing in the thought of God as the church of the Chinese, but there is such a thing as the church of the Pekinese. Scripture knows nothing of the church of the French, but it does recognize the church of the Parisians. A clear apprehension of the divine basis of church formation—according to the difference of cities and not of countries—will save us from the misconception of the indigenous church. There should be no distinction whatever between Chinese and foreign Christians, between Chinese and foreign workers, or between Chinese and foreign money in any given locality.

(7) SOCIAL DISTINCTIONS. In Paul's day, from a social point of view, there was a great gulf fixed between a free man and a slave; yet they worshipped side by side in the same church. In our day, if a rickshaw coolie and the president of our republic both belong to Christ and live in the same place, then they belong to the same church. There may be a mission for rickshaw coolies, but there can never be a church for rickshaw coolies. *Social distinctions are no adequate basis for forming a separate church. In the Church of God there "cannot be slave nor free man."*

In Scripture we have at least seven definite things referred to which are forbidden by God as reasons for dividing His Church. As a matter of fact these seven points are only typical of all other reasons the human mind may devise for dividing the Church of God. The two millenniums of Church history are a sad record of human inventions to destroy the Church's oneness.

OVERCOMERS

The sphere of the church is local, and the local church should on no account be divided. The question naturally arises, if the spiritual life of a local *(not denominational)* church is very low, can a few of the more spiritual members not gather together and form another assembly? The answer from the Word of God is emphatically, No! God's Word only warrants the establishment of churches on local ground. Even lack of spirituality is no adequate reason for dividing the church. Should local methods, government, and organization be far from ideal, that still constitutes no reason for division. Even wrong teaching (2 John 9 excepted) is no ground for those who know better to form a separate church. We must lay it to heart that the difference of locality *is the only ground for dividing the Church of God.* No other ground is scriptural.

We who live in the same locality cannot but belong to the same church. This is something from which there is no escape. If I am dissatisfied with the local church, the only thing I can do is to change my locality; then automatically I change my church. *We can leave a denomination, but we can never leave a church.* To leave a sect is justifiable, but to leave a church—whether on account of unspirituality, wrong doctrine, or bad organization—is utterly unjustifiable. If you leave the local church and form a separate assembly, you may have greater spirituality, purer teaching, and better government; but *you have no church;* you have only a sect.

In the second and third chapters of Revelation we see seven different churches in seven different localities. Only two were not rebuked but actually praised by the Lord. The other five were all definitely censured. Spiritually those five were in a sad state. They were weak, defeated churches; but they were churches for all that, not sects. Spiritually they were wrong, but positionally they were right; therefore, God only commanded those in them to be *overcomers.* The Lord said not a word about leaving the church. A local church is a church which you cannot leave; you must remain in it. If you are more spiritual than the other members, then you should use your spiritual influence and your authority in prayer to revive that church. If the church does not respond, you have only two alternatives; you must either remain there, keeping yourself undefiled, or else you must change your dwelling place. *But this does not apply to a sect.* It is futile to seek by a wrong application of these two chapters to keep Spirit-taught believers within a sect, for the seven churches referred to are *local churches,* not sectarian "churches." However weak they may have been, they were still on the scriptural ground of the Body in the locality. The Word of God has never authorized anyone to leave a church. All groups of believers who base their fellowship on other ground than that of locality are sects, even though they may term themselves churches. It is all right to leave a sect, but it is never right to leave a local church. If you leave a local church, you do so without the authority of the Lord, and you become guilty of the sin of schism in the Body.

What a tragedy it is when a few spiritual members leave a local church, and form another assembly, simply because the other members are weak and immature. Those stronger members should remain in that church as overcomers, seeking to help their weaker brothers and sisters, and claiming the situation there for the Lord. Oh, how prone we are to despise the believers we consider inferior to us, and how we delight to associate with those whose fellowship we find specially congenial. Pride of heart, and a selfish enjoyment in spiritual things, causes us to overlook the fact that a church in any given place should consist of all the children of God in that place; so we narrow down Christian fellowship and make selection among the children of God. This is sectarianism, and it is a grief of heart to the Lord.

CHAPTER SIX

THE WORK AND THE CHURCHES

THE APOSTLES AND THE CHURCHES

In regard to the universal Church, God first brought it into being, and thereafter set apostles to minister to it (1 Cor. 12:28); but in regard to the local churches the order was quite otherwise. The appointment of apostles preceded the founding of local churches. Our Lord *first* commissioned the twelve apostles, and *thereafter* the church in Jerusalem came into existence. The Holy Spirit *first* called two apostles—Paul and Barnabas—to the work, and *thereafter* a number of churches sprang into being in different places. So it is clear that the apostolic ministry *precedes* the existence of the local churches, and consequently it is obvious that the work of apostles does not belong to the local churches.

As we have already observed, the Holy Spirit said, "Set apart for Me now Barnabas and Saul for *the work* to which I have called them." The service that followed the apostles' separation, which we generally refer to as their missionary campaigns, the Holy Spirit referred to as "the work." "The work" was the object of the Spirit's call, and all that was accomplished by Paul and his associates in the days and years that followed, all that for which they were responsible, was included in this one term, "the work." (The term "the work" is used in a specific sense in this book, and relates to all that is included in the missionary efforts of the apostles.)

Since churches are the result of the work, they cannot possibly include it. If we are to understand the mind of God concerning His work, then we must differentiate clearly between the work and the churches. These two are quite distinct in Scripture, and we must avoid confusing them; otherwise we shall make serious mistakes, and the outworking of God's purposes will be hindered. The word "churches" appears frequently in Scripture, so it has been easy for us to arrive at a clear understanding of its meaning and content, but the word "work" is not often used in the specific sense in which it is employed here, with the result that we have paid little heed to it. But the Spirit has used the expression in an inclusive way to cover all that related to the purpose of the apostolic call. Let us then abide by the term which the Spirit has chosen to employ.

It has been repeated again and again, but let us point it out once again, that the churches are local, and nothing outside the locality must interfere with them, nor must they interfere with anything beyond that sphere. Church affairs are to be managed by local men who, on account of their comparative spiritual maturity, have been appointed to be elders. As the work of the apostles is to preach the gospel and found churches, not to take responsibility in the churches already established, their office is not a church office. If they go to work in a place where no church exists, then they should seek to found one by the proclamation of the gospel; but if one exists already, then their work must be distinct from it. In the will of God "the church" and "the work" follow two distinct lines.

The work belongs to the apostles, while the churches belong to the local believers. The apostles are responsible for the work in any place, and the church is responsible for all the children of God there. In the matter of church fellowship the apostles regard themselves as the *brethren* of all believers in the city, but in the matter of work, they regard themselves as its personnel, and maintain a distinction between themselves and the church. As members of the Body, they meet for mutual edification with all their fellow members in the locality; but as ministering members of the Body, their specific ministry constitutes them a group of workers apart from the church. It is wrong for the apostles to interfere with the affairs of the church, but it is equally wrong for the church to interfere with the affairs of the work. The apostles manage the work; the elders manage the church. It follows then that we must be clear about our call. Has God called us to be elders, or to be apostles? If elders, then our responsibility is confined to local affairs; if apostles, then our responsibility is extra-local. If elders, then our sphere is the church; if apostles, then our sphere lies beyond the church, in the work. The reason God called apostles and entrusted the work to them is that He wished to preserve the local character of the church. If any church exercises control over work in another locality, it at once becomes extra-local, and thereby loses its specific characteristic as a church. The responsibility of the work in different places is committed to apostles, whose sphere extends beyond the locality. The responsibility of the church is committed to elders, whose sphere is confined to the locality. An Ephesian elder is an elder in Ephesus, but he ceases to be an elder when he comes to Philippi, and *vice versa*. Eldership is limited to locality. When Paul was at Miletus, he wished to see the representative members of the church in Ephesus, so he sent for the Ephesian elders. But no request was sent to the Ephesian apostle, for the simple reason that there was none. The apostles belong to different places, not to one place alone, whereas the sphere of the elders is strictly local, for which reason they take no official responsibility beyond the place in which they live. Whenever the church tries to control the work, the church loses its local character. Whenever an apostle tries to control a church, he loses his extra-local character. Much confusion has arisen because the divine line of demarcation between the churches and the work has been lost sight of.

RESPONSIBILITY—SPIRITUAL AND OFFICIAL

Just as the apostles have *spiritual* but no *official* responsibility regarding the church, so the elders, and the whole church, have *spiritual* but no *official* responsibility regarding the work. It is commendable if a local church seeks to help in the work; but it is under no official obligation to do so. If the members of the church are spiritual, they cannot but regard the work of God as their work, in which case they will count it a joy to help in any way. They will recognize that, while the official responsibility for the work rests on the apostles, the spiritual responsibility is shared by all the children of God, and consequently by them. *There is a vast difference between spiritual and official responsibility.* In the matter of official responsibility there are certain prescribed duties, and one is in the wrong if one fails to perform them. But in the matter of spiritual responsibility there are no legal obligations. Therefore, any neglect of responsibility does not register as an official shortcoming, but it does register as a low spiritual state. From an official point of view, the responsibility of the work rests upon the apostles. If they lack the needed help, they cannot demand it; but if the church is spiritual, its members will see the meaning of the Body and will gladly assist in the work and give towards it. If the church fails in spiritual responsibility, the apostles may have difficulties which they should not have, and the church will suffer spiritually. On the other hand, the responsibility of the church rests officially upon the elders; therefore, the apostles should not take upon themselves to do anything directly there. They may and should assist the church by their counsel and exhortations. If the local believers are spiritual, they will willingly receive such help; but should they be unspiritual, and in consequence reject the help the apostles offer, their failure is spiritual and not official, and the apostles have no option but to leave them to their own resources. The church does not come within the sphere of the work and is consequently outside the sphere of their authority. Again let us repeat, the churches are local, intensely local; the work is extra-local, and always extra-local.

REPRESENTATIVES OF THE MINISTRY OF THE BODY—INDIVIDUALS, NOT CHURCHES

There is a definite divine reason for the fact that the work is entrusted to individual apostles and not to local churches; but before we enter into that, let us examine the fundamental difference between the activities of a church as a body and the activities of a brother as an individual. It may be all right for a brother (or for several brothers) to go into business, but it would be all wrong for a church to do so. It might be quite in order for one or more brothers to open a restaurant or a hotel, but that would not be in order for a church. What may be perfectly permissible in the case of brothers, as individuals, is not necessarily permissible in the case of a church, as a company. The business of the churches consists in the *mutual* care of their various members, such as the conduct of meetings for breaking of bread, for the exercise of spiritual gifts, for the study of the Word, for prayer, for fellowship, and for gospel preaching. The work is beyond the sphere of any church as *a* corporate body; it is the responsibility of individuals, though *not of individuals as such.*

There is no scriptural precedent for such work being undertaken by a church, as, for instance, hospitals, or schools, or even something on a more definitely spiritual plane such as foreign missions. It is perfectly in order for one or more members of a church to run a hospital, or a school, or to be responsible for mission work, but not for any church as a whole. A church exists for the purpose of mutual help in one place, not for the purpose of bearing the responsibility of work in different places. According to God's Word, all the work is the personal concern of individual brothers called and commissioned by God, *as members of the Body,* and not the concern of any church as a body. The responsibility of the work is always borne by one or more individuals.

The important point to note is that the Body of Christ in its ministry aspect is not represented by local churches, but by *individuals* who are the gifts given by God to His Church. A local church has not been chosen by God to represent the Body *where ministry is in view.* When God wants any representatives of the Body to express its ministry, He chooses certain individuals, who are the functioning members, to represent that Body. The whole thing is clear in the last part of 1 Corinthians 12.

It was never the thought of God that His work should be done on any other basis than that of the Body, because it is actually the natural functioning of the Body of Christ. It is the activity, under the direction of the Head, of those members who possess special faculties. We have already pointed out that the local church represents the Body in its life aspect, and the functioning members represent the Body in its ministry aspect. The local church is called to manifest not so much the service, as the life of the Body, while the apostles, prophets, and teachers, as such, are called to manifest not so much the life, as the service of the Body. That is the reason God did not entrust the work to any local church as a body, but to individuals. But it is the latter, not the former, who represent the Body, if the latter are functioning members of the Body.

Therefore, we find that the two apostles who went out from Antioch were not sent forth to the work by the *whole church* but by *several ministers in the church,* because in the matter of service and work it is the latter, not the former, who represent the Body. So the work is the responsibility of individuals who are called and commissioned by God, and not the responsibility of the whole church.

But, let it be clearly understood, by individuals we do not mean individuals as individuals, but as functioning members *representing the Body.* God has never sanctioned that anyone take up an individualistic line in His work. Free-lancing, without due coordination with other members of the Body, has never been a divine manner of work. This cannot be too strongly emphasized; nor can it be too strongly emphasized that in His work God uses individuals to represent the Body, not local churches. Therefore, while the work is the responsibility of individuals, it is not the business of just any individual who cares to take it up, but only of such as are called and sent forth by God, and are equipped with spiritual gifts for the task. Only those who represent the ministry of the Body can bear the official responsibility of the work. The work *is* undertaken by individuals, but only by such as represent the Body in its ministry aspect, for they, not the entire church, are responsible for it. It is not individuals, as individuals, that undertake the work, but individuals as representing the Body of Christ.

If our work is that of an apostle, it must be clearly distinguished from the local church. It may seem quite unimportant to some that any distinction be made between the work and the church. They may think it of no consequence that the responsibility of the work be in the hands of individual members, not the whole church, and that the apostles be responsible only for the work, not for the church; but the principle is a scriptural principle, and its outworking is of great importance and has tremendous effects, as we shall presently see.

"HIS OWN RENTED DWELLING"

The church in Rome is a good illustration of the foregoing. Before Paul visited Rome, he had written to the church there expressing an intense desire to see them (Rom. 1:10-11). From his letter it is obvious that a church had been established in that city prior to his arrival. When he actually reached Rome, the church there did not hand over local responsibility to him, nor did they say (as a church today probably would), "Now that an apostle has come into our midst, he must take over the responsibility and be our pastor." Instead, we find this amazing record in the Word: "And he remained two whole years in his own rented dwelling and welcomed all those who came to him, proclaiming the kingdom of God and teaching the things concerning the Lord Jesus Christ with all boldness, unhindered" (Acts 28:30-31). Why did Paul live in "his own rented dwelling" and preach and teach from there and not from the already existing church? Some may suggest that because he was a prisoner he would not have been allowed to take meetings in the church; but there would have been little difference between taking meetings in the church and in the house. If he was granted permission to rent a house and preach and teach there, why should he have been refused permission to preach and teach in connection with the church? Moreover, we need to remember that the Word does *not* state the *reason* Paul rented a house and preached and taught there; it *only* mentions the *fact*. The fact is that he did rent a house and did preach and teach there, and that fact is enough for us. It is enough for our guidance. Further, God has made it clear that he was under no necessity to do so. No pressure whatever was brought to bear upon him, for he acted "with all boldness unhindered."

Then what is the meaning of the rented house? We must remember the divine economy of words in Scripture, and we must realize that neither the occurrence, nor the record of it, was accidental. There is no room for chance happenings or unimportant records in God's Word. All that is written there is written for our learning, and even a seemingly casual remark may enfold a precious lesson. Moreover, this book is the book of the Acts of the Apostles, who moved under the direct guidance of the Holy Spirit, so the record in question is also one of the acts of the apostles, and is therefore not a chance happening, but an act under the guidance of the Holy Spirit. Here in two short sentences we have an important principle, namely, that the apostolic work and the local church are quite distinct. A church had already been established in Rome; therefore, the members must have had at least one meeting place, *but they did not request that Paul take control of the local church, nor did they make their place of meeting Paul's center of work*. Paul had his own work in his own rented house quite apart from the church, and apart from their meeting place, and he did not take over the responsibility of the local church affairs.

Every apostle must learn to live in "his own rented dwelling" and work with that as his center, leaving the responsibility of the local church to the local brethren.[1] The work of God belongs to the workers, but the church of God belongs to the locality. Any work in a given place is only temporary, but any church in a given place is always permanent. The work is movable; the church is stationary. When God indicates that an apostle should move, his work moves with him, but the church remains. When Paul thought of leaving Corinth, the Lord showed him He had further ministry for him in the city, so Paul remained for eighteen months — not permanently. When Paul left Corinth, his work left, but the church in Corinth continued, although the fruits of his work were left in the church. A church should not be influenced by the movements of the workers. Whether they are present or absent, the church should move steadily forward. Every one of God's workmen must have a clean-cut

---

[1] Note: This does not mean that an apostle will not go into a local church and minister. See pp. 179-180.

line of demarcation between his work and the church in the place of his labors.

The work of the apostles and the work of the local church run parallel; they do not converge. When the apostles are working in any place, their work goes on side by side with the work of the church. The two never coincide, nor can the one ever be a substitute for the other. On leaving a place, an apostle should hand over all the fruit of his work to the local church. It is not God's will that the work of an apostle should take the place of the work of the church, or be in any wise identified with it.

The principle of Paul living in his own rented house shows clearly that the work of the church is unaffected by the presence or absence of an apostle. After Paul's arrival in Rome, the work of the church went on as before, independently of him. Since it was dependent on him neither for its origin nor its continuance, it would be unaffected by his departure. Work is work, and church is church, and these two lines never converge, but keep running parallel one to the other.

Suppose we go to Kweiyang to work; what should be our procedure? On arrival in Kweiyang we either live in an inn, or rent a room, and we begin to preach the gospel. When men are saved, what shall we do? We must encourage them to read the Word, to pray, to give, to witness, and to assemble for fellowship and ministry. One of the tragic mistakes of the past hundred years of foreign missions in China (God be merciful to me if I say anything amiss!) is that after a worker led men to Christ, he prepared a place and invited them to come there for meetings, instead of encouraging them to assemble by themselves. Efforts have been made to encourage the young believers to read the Word *themselves,* pray by *themselves,* witness *themselves,* but never to *meet by themselves.* Workers never think of reading, praying, and witnessing for them, but they do not see any harm in arranging meetings for them. We need to show the new converts that such duties as reading, praying, witnessing, giving, *and assembling together* are the minimum requirement of Christians. We should teach them to have *their own* meetings in *their own* meeting place. Let us say to them,

"Just as we cannot read the Word, or pray, or witness for you, so we cannot take the responsibility of preparing a meeting place for you and leading your meetings. You must seek out suitable premises and conduct your own meetings. *Your* meetings are *your* responsibility, and a regular assembling of yourselves is one of your chief duties and privileges."

Many workers regard their meetings and the meetings of the church as one and the same thing, but they are not. (See chapter nine.) Therefore, as soon as a few believers are saved, we must instruct them to take full responsibility for their private reading, prayer, and witness, and also for the public meetings of the church.

As for ourselves, while we go on working and keep our work distinct from the work of the church, we must go and have fellowship with the believers in *their* various local gatherings. We must go and break bread with them, join with them in the exercise of spiritual gifts, and take part in their prayer meetings. When there is no church in the place to which God has sent us, we are only workers there, but as soon as there is a local church, we are brothers as well as workers. In our capacity as workers we can take no responsibility in the local church, but in our capacity as local brothers we go and meet with all the members of the church as their *fellow* members.

As soon as there is a local church in the place of our labors, we automatically become members. Here is the chief point to observe in the relationship between the church and the work—the worker must leave the believers to initiate and conduct their own meetings in their own meeting place, and then he must go to *them* and take part in *their* meetings, not ask them to come to *him* and take part in *his* meetings. Otherwise, we shall become settlers in one place and shall change our office from apostle to pastor; then when we eventually leave, we shall have to find a successor to carry out the church work. If we keep "church" and "work" parallel and do not let the two lines converge, we shall find that no adjustment will be needed in the church when we depart, for it will not have lost a "pastor," but only a brother. Unless we differentiate clearly in our own minds between church and work, we shall mix the work with the church and the church with the work; there will be confusion in both directions, and the growth both of the church and the work will be arrested.

"Self-government, self-support, and self-propagation" has been the slogan of many workers for a number of years now. The need to deal with these matters has arisen because of the confusion between the church and the work. In a mission, when people are saved, then the missionaries prepare a hall for them, arrange for prayer meetings and Bible classes, and some of them go as far as to manage the business and spiritual affairs of the church as well. The mission does the work of the local church! Therefore, it is not surprising that in the process of time, problems arise in connection with self-government, self-support, and self-propagation. In the very nature of things, such problems would never have come up for consideration if the principles shown us in God's Word had been adhered to from the very beginning.

Anyone who cares enough to be a Christian ought to be taught from the outset what the implications are. Believers must pray *themselves,* study the Word *themselves,* and assemble *themselves,* not merely go to a meeting place prepared *by others* and sit down and listen to *others* preach. Going to a mission compound or a mission hall to hear the Word is not scriptural assembling, because it is in the hands of a missionary, or of his mission, not in the hands of the local church. It is a mixture of work and church. If from the outset Christians learned to gather together according to the Scriptures, many problems would be avoided.

THE RESULTS OF THE WORK

When a servant of God reaches a new place, his first business must be to found a local church, unless there is one already in existence, in which case his one concern must be to help the church. The one aim of the work in any place is the building up of the church in that place. All the fruit of a worker's labors must go to the increase of the church. The work in any place exists for the church alone, not for itself. The apostle's goal is to build up the church, not to build up his work or any group of people that may have sent him out.

Wherein lies the failure of missions today? They keep the results of their work in their own hands. In other words, they have reckoned *their* converts as members of *their* mission, or of *their* mission church, instead of building them into, or handing them over, to the local churches. The result is that the mission extends all the while and becomes quite an imposing organization, but local churches are scarcely to be found. And because there are no local churches, the mission has to send workers to different places as "pastors" of the various companies of Christians. So church is not church, and work is not work, but both are a medley of the two. There seems to be no scriptural warrant for forming companies of workers into missions; nevertheless, to regard a mission as an apostolic company is not definitely unscriptural, but for missions to enlarge their own organization instead of establishing local churches is distinctly so.

TWO LINES OF WORK

An apostle should go and work in a certain place if the local church invites him, or if he himself has received a revelation from the Lord to work there. In the latter case, if there is a church in the place, he can write notifying them of his coming, just as Paul notified the churches in Corinth and in Rome. These are the two lines which regulate the work of an apostle—he must either have a direct revelation of God's will, or an indirect revelation through the invitation of a church.

Wherever an apostle goes, he must learn to bear his own responsibility, having his own rented dwelling. It may be all right to work in a place, living as the guest of the local church, but it would not be right to impose upon them by taking advantage of their hospitality over an extended period. If a worker expects to stay for any length of time in one place, then he must have his own center of work, and he must not only bear his own personal responsibilities, but also all responsibilities in connection with the work. A local church must bear entire responsibility for *its* own work, and so must the worker for *his*. The church as such must not be involved in any financial outlay in connection with the work; the worker alone is liable for all expenses incurred, and he must learn from the very outset of his ministry to look to the Lord for the supply of his needs. Of course, if the church is spiritual, its members will recognize their spiritual responsibility, and will be willing to assist in material ways so that the work of God may go forward, but the worker should take nothing for granted and should bear the entire financial burden, so that it may be manifest that the church and the work are absolutely distinct.

When an apostle comes to a place where a local church already exists, he must never forget that no church authority rests with him. Should he desire to work in a place where the local church does not wish to have him, then all he can do is to pass on to some other part. The church has full authority either to receive or reject a worker. Even should the worker in question have been used of God to found the very church that rejects him, he can claim no authority in the church on that account.

Should he know unmistakably that God has led him to work in that place, yet the local church refuse to welcome him, if they persist in their attitude, then he must obey the command of God and go and work there despite them. But he must not gather believers around him, nor must he on any account form a separate church. There can only be one church in one place. If he forms a separate company of believers where a local church already exists, he will be forming a sect and not a church. Churches are founded on the ground of locality, not on the ground of receiving a certain apostle. Even if the local church refused to receive him, and his work had to be done without its sympathy and cooperation, or even despite its opposition, still all the results of his labors must be for their benefit. Despite its attitude toward the apostle personally, all the fruit of his labors must be contributed to that church. The sole aim of all work for God is the increase and up-building of the local churches. If they welcome the worker, the result of his labors goes to them; if they reject him, it goes to them just the same.

We require deeper spiritual experience and clearer spiritual light if we are to be workers acceptable to God and to

His Church. If we wish to overcome difficulties, we must learn to overcome by spirituality, not by official authority. If we are spiritual, we shall submit to the authority of the local churches. It is lack of submission on the part of God's servants that is responsible for the forming of numerous sects. Many so-called churches have been established because workers have been rejected by the churches and have gathered groups of people around them, who have supported them and the doctrines they taught. Such a procedure is sectarian.

If we are truly led of God, surely we can trust God to open doors for us. If a church receives us, let us praise Him; if not, let us look confidently to Him to unlock closed doors. Many servants of God trust Him to open up spiritual truths to them, but they cannot trust Him to open doors for the reception of those truths. They have faith to believe God will give them light, but they have no faith to believe that He will also supply the keys to open human hearts to the light He has given. So they resort to carnal methods, and the consequence is much division among the children of God. If God Himself does not remove the obstacles in our circumstances, then we must quietly remain where we are, and not have recourse to natural means, which will assuredly work havoc in the Church of God.

THE SPECIFIC MINISTRIES OF THE WORD

All God's servants are engaged in the ministry of building up the Body of Christ, but it does not follow that, because all are in the ministry of the Word, all ministries are the same. Everyone has a different line of ministry. Time and again God has raised up some new witness, or group of witnesses, giving them fresh light from His Word, so that they could bear a special testimony for Him in the particular time and circumstances in which they live. All such ministry is new and specific and is of great value to the Church; but we must bear it well in mind that if God commits a specific ministry to any man relating to certain truths, he must not make his particular ministry, or his particular line of truth, the basis of a new "church." No servant of God should cherish the ambition that his truth be accepted as *the* truth. If doors are closed to it, let him wait patiently upon God who gave it until He opens doors for its reception. No separate "church" must be formed to bear a separate testimony. The work of God does not sanction the establishment of a church for the propagation of any particular line of teaching. It knows only one kind of church—the local church; not a sectarian church, but a New Testament church.

Let us lay it to heart that *our work is for our ministry and our ministry is for the churches*. No church should be under a specific ministry, but all ministries should be under the church. What havoc has been wrought in the Church because so many of her ministers have sought to bring the churches under their ministry, rather than by their ministry serve the churches. As soon as the churches are brought under any ministry, they cease to be local and become sectarian.

When a specific ministry has been raised up of God to meet a specific need in His Church, what should be the attitude of the minister? Whenever a new truth is proclaimed, it will have new followers. The worker to whom God has given fresh light upon His truth should encourage all who receive that truth to swell the ranks of the local church, not to range themselves around him. Otherwise, the churches will be made to serve the ministry, not the ministry the churches, and the "churches" established will be ministerial "churches," not local ones. The sphere of a church is not the sphere of any ministry, but the sphere of the locality. Wherever ministry is made the occasion for the forming of a church, there you have the beginning of a new denomination. From the study of Church history we can see that almost all new ministries have led to new followings, and new followings have resulted in new organizations. Thus ministerial "churches" have been established and denominations multiplied.

If the Lord delays His coming and His servants remain true to Him, He will certainly raise up new ministries in the Word. He will open up special truths to meet the specific needs of His children. Some of the hearers will question the truths, others reject them, and others condemn, while there will be those who gladly respond. What should the attitude of God's servants be? They must be fully persuaded in their own minds that *there can only be one church in one place,* and that all truth is for the enrichment of that church. If it receives the truths God's ministers proclaim, let them praise Him; if not, let them praise Him still. No thought must be entertained of forming a separate "church" comprising those believers who support the special doctrines emphasized. If in the local church a number of people receive their teaching, *then they must still remain there.* No divisive work must be done in the local church. Those who receive the truth may use their spiritual teaching and spiritual power to help their fellow members, but they must not use any divisive methods to support the truth they have embraced. If we always bear in mind that the churches of God are only formed on the basis of locality, much division among the children of God will be avoided.

Should God entrust us with a special ministry and lead us to a place where no church exists, our first duty is to establish one in the locality, and then contribute our ministry to it. We can establish local churches and contribute our ministry to such churches, but we dare not establish ministerial churches.

Let me illustrate the relation between various ministries and various local churches. One man is a florist, another a grocer. The most obvious way for them to extend their business is to establish branches in various districts. The florist opens branch shops to sell flowers, and the grocer opens branch shops to sell groceries. This is just like the various ministers trying to establish "churches" according to their ministry. God's plan for His Church is on quite a different line. It is not that the grocer and the florist each seek to open as many branches as they possibly can in order to sell their respective commodities, but that the grocer or the florist, arriving in any place, opens a department store, and having duly established that, he contributes his goods to it, and other tradesmen coming along contribute their wares to the same store. A department store does not just deal in one line of goods; it has a varied stock. The thought of God is not that we should open branch florist shops or branch grocery stores, or stores that specialize in other lines, but department stores. His plan is that His servants should just establish a local church, and then contribute their different ministries to that church. The church is not controlled by *one* ministry but served by *all* the ministries. If any company of God's people are open to receive one truth only, then they are a sect.

As apostles our first concern on arrival in a place which has no church is to found one there. As soon as it has been formed, we should seek to serve it with whatever ministry the Lord has entrusted to us, and then leave it. We dare to exercise our ministry faithfully, but having done so, we dare to leave the church open to other ministry. This should be the attitude of all God's workmen. We should never cherish the hope that only "our" teaching will be accepted by any church. There must be no thought of dominating a church by our personality or by our ministry; the field must be left clear for all God's servants. There is no need to build a wall of protection around "our" particular "flock" to secure them *against* the teachings of others. If we do so, we are working along popish lines. We can safely trust God to protect our ministry, and we must remember that for "the perfecting of the saints" the varied ministries of all God's faithful servants are necessary. Local responsibility is with the elders; *they* must watch the interests of the flock in the matter of ministries.

INSTITUTIONS OF FAITH

It must not be inferred from the foregoing that God has no other workmen but apostles and the various ministers of the Word. Those who work in the ministry of the Word are only a section of God's servants. The work is not the only work. God has many servants who are bearing the burden of various works of faith, such as schools, orphanages, and hospitals. Looked at superficially, their work does not seem as spiritual as the work of the apostles or ministers we have just referred to, but in reality it is. Although such faith workers do not go forth as apostles, or teach the Word like the special ministers, yet they are used just as definitely as the others to strengthen the Church of God.

George Müller's orphanage is just such a faith work. It has resulted in the salvation of many souls. The question arises, where should the fruits of such a work go? Not into an orphanage "church," but into the local church. A work such as that is not a unit sufficiently large to form a church. It is the city which is a church unit, not an institution. No matter how prosperous a work of faith may be, and no matter how many souls may be saved through it, no church can be formed on such a basis; for should there be various workers in one city engaged in various kinds of work, then there would be as many churches as there were such institutions. The boundary of a church is a city, not any institution in a city.

Several years ago I was in Tsinan. Some brothers in Cheloo University asked me if I thought it time for them to begin a meeting for the breaking of bread. I asked, "Do you represent Cheloo University or Tsinan city?" They answered, "Cheloo." "Then I do not think it is right," I said. Of course, they wanted to know why, so I explained: "The Word of God sanctions the forming of a church in Tsinan, but not in Cheloo. The sphere of Cheloo is too narrow to justify the existence of a separate church. The standard scriptural unit for the forming of a church is a city, not a university."

The fruits resulting from various institutions of faith must not be retained by such institutions. All must be handed over to the local church. Workers must not argue that because they have been the means of salvation to certain souls, therefore they have a special claim upon them and special responsibility for them, and consequently withhold them from uniting with their fellow believers in the locality. Even though there may be regular prayers, and preaching, and a variety of meetings in connection with a Christian institution, those can never serve as a substitute for church fellowship, and no such institution, however spiritual, can be regarded as a church, since it is not founded on the divinely appointed basis of locality. All Christians engaged in efforts of this kind must differentiate clearly between church and work, and they must realize that any sphere narrower than a locality does not justify the forming of a separate church. They dare not pride themselves on their successful work and think it will serve well as a church, but they must humbly join in fellowship with all the other members of the Body of Christ in the place where they live.

All the various God-given ministries have one aim, the establishing of local churches. In the thought of God only one company of people exists, and all His designs of grace center in that one company—His Church. The work is not a goal in itself; it is only a means to an end. If we regard our work as an end, then our purpose is at variance with God's, for His end is the Church. What we regard as an end in itself is only the means to His end.

There are three things which we must bear clearly in mind. (1) The work and other works are the special concern of the workers, not of the churches, and the sphere of any work is not wide enough to justify its being regarded as a church. (2) All workers must be humble enough to take the place of brothers in the local church. In the sphere of their work they hold the position of God's servants, but in the sphere of the church they are only brethren. In the church there are only children of God; therefore, none of its members are "workers," all are brethren. (3) The goal of all work is the establishment of local churches. If we make our work the basis of a separate unit of God's people, then we are building up a sect, not a church.

CHAPTER SEVEN

AMONG THE WORKERS

The churches in Scripture are intensely local. We never find any federation of churches there; they are all independent units. The position is quite otherwise as regards the workers. Among them we find a certain amount of association; we see here a little group, and there another, linked together for the work. Paul and those with him—as for instance Luke, Silas, Timothy, Titus, and Apollos—formed one group. Peter, James, John, and those with them formed another. One group came out from Antioch, another from Jerusalem. Paul refers to those who were with him (Acts 20:34), which indicates that while there was no organization of the workers into different missions, still they had their own special associates in the work. Even in the beginning, when our Lord chose the twelve, He sent them out two by two. *All* were fellow workers, but *each* had his special fellow worker. Such grouping of workers was ordained and ordered by the Lord.

These apostolic companies were not formed along partisan or doctrinal lines; they were formed under the sovereignty of the Spirit, who so ordered the circumstances of the different workers as to link them together in the work. It was not that they were really divided from other workers, but merely that in the Spirit's ordering of their ways, they had not been led into special association with them. It was the Holy Spirit, not men, who said, "Set apart for Me now Barnabas and Saul." Everything hinged on the sovereignty of the Spirit. The apostolic companies were subject to the will and ordering of the Lord. As we have seen, the twelve were divided into pairs, but it was not left to their personal discretion to choose their associates; it was the Lord who coupled them together and sent them forth. Each had a special fellow worker, but that fellow worker was of the Lord's appointing, not of their choosing. It was not because of natural affinity that they associated specially with some, nor was it because of difference in doctrine or practice that they did not associate specially with others. The deciding factor was *always* the ordering of the Lord.

We recognize that the Lord is the Head of the Church, and that the apostles were the first order "placed" by the Lord in the Church (1 Cor. 12:28). Although they were formed into associations, having their special fellow workers appointed by the Lord, still they had no special name, system, or organization. They did not make a company smaller than the Body to be the basis of their work; all was on the ground of the Body. Therefore, although on account of difference of locality and the providential ordering of their ways, they formed different groups, still they had no organization outside the Body; their work was always an expression of the ministry of the Body. They were constituted into separate companies, but each company stood on the ground of the Body, expressing the ministry of the Body.

The Lord is the Head of the Body and *not the Head of any organization;* therefore, whenever we work for a society, a mission, or an institution, and not for the Body alone, we lose the headship of the Lord. We must see clearly that the work is the work of the Body of Christ and that, while the Lord did divide His workers into different companies (not different organizations), their work was always on the ground of the Body. And we must recognize that every individual worker and every company represents the ministry of the Body of Christ, each office held being held in the Body, and for the furtherance of the work of God. Then, and only then, can we have one ministry—the up-building of the Body of Christ. If we recognized clearly the oneness of the Body, what blessed results we should see! Wherever the principle of the oneness of the Body operates, all possibility of rivalry is ruled out. It does not matter if I decrease and you increase; there will neither be jealousy on my part, nor pride on yours. Once we see that all the work and all its fruits are for the increase of the Body of Christ, then no man will be counted yours and no man mine; it will not matter then whether you are used or I. All carnal strife among the workers of God will be at an end once the Body is clearly seen as the principle of the work. But life and work in the Body necessitate drastic dealings with the flesh, and that in turn necessitates a deep knowledge of the cross of Christ.

The early apostles were never free lances; they worked together. In the story of Pentecost we read of "Peter, standing with the eleven" (Acts 2:14). At the Beautiful Gate we see Peter and John working together, and again they were the two who visited Samaria. When Peter went to the house of Cornelius, six other brothers accompanied him. When the apostles went out, it was always in companies, or at least by twos, never alone. Their work was not individual, but corporate. As to those with Paul at Antioch and elsewhere, it is unfortunate that so much emphasis has been placed upon Paul as an individual, with the result that his fellow workers are almost lost sight of. We see that at Troas, Luke joined their company and was of one mind with Paul in considering that the Macedonian cry should be responded to. Later on when they returned from Macedonia, they brought with them as fellow workers Sopater, Aristarchus, Secundus, Gaius, Timothy, Tychicus, and Trophimus. Later on we find Apollos, Priscilla, and Aquila joining them. Still later we find Paul sending Timothy to Corinth and encouraging Apollos and Titus to go there; and some time afterwards we see Epaphroditus joining them as a fellow worker. And it is good to read at the head of Paul's Epistles words like these: "Paul... and Sosthenes the brother," "Paul...and Timothy the brother," "Paul...Silas and Timothy."

So we see no trace of organized missions in Scripture on the one hand, nor do we see any workers going out on individual lines on the other hand, each being a law to himself. They are formed into companies, but such companies are on a spiritual basis, not on the basis of organization. Scripture gives no warrant for an organized mission on the one hand, nor does it sanction free-lance work on the other hand; the one is as far from the thought of God as the other. Therefore, while we must guard against the snare of man-made organizations, we must also guard against the danger of being too individualistic. We must not be organized into a mission and thus become schismatic; at the same time we must have associates in the work with whom we cooperate on a spiritual basis, and thus maintain the testimony of the Body.

We need to emphasize this fact, that the apostles worked in association with others, but their companies were not organized. Their relationship one to another was only spiritual. They loved and served the same Lord, they had one call and one commission, and they were of one mind. The Lord united them; therefore, they became fellow workers. Some were together from the outset; others joined at a later date. They were one company, yet they had no organization, and there was no distribution of offices or positions. Those who joined them did not come in response to some "Help Wanted" advertisement, nor did they come because they were equipped by a special course of training. On their journeys the Lord so ordered circumstances that they met; He drew them one to another, and being of one mind and one spirit, linked together by the Lord, they spontaneously became fellow workers. In order to join such a company there was no need of first passing an examination, or of fulfilling some special conditions, or of going through certain forms or ceremonies. The Lord was the One who determined everything. He ordered; man only concurred. In such groups none held special positions or offices; there was no director, or chairman, or superintendent. Whatever ministry the Lord had given them, that constituted their position. *They received no appointments from the association.* The relationship which existed between its members was purely spiritual, not official. They were constituted fellow workers, not by a human organization, but by a spiritual bond.

SPIRITUAL AUTHORITY

Before considering the question of spiritual authority, let us read a few passages of Scripture bearing on the relationship between the workers, as they throw considerable light on our subject. "Timothy...Paul wanted this one to go forth with him" (Acts 16:1-3). "When he [Paul] had seen the vision, *we* immediately endeavored to go forth into Macedonia, *concluding* that God had called us to announce the gospel to them" (Acts 16:10). "And those who conducted Paul brought him as far as Athens; and receiving a *command* for Silas and Timothy to come to him as quickly as possible, they went off" (Acts 17:15). Paul "*resolved* to return through Macedonia. And Sopater of Berea, the son of Pyrrhus, accompanied him" (Acts 20:3-4). "We, going ahead onto the ship, set sail for Assos, from there intending to pick up Paul, for so he had *arranged*" (Acts 20:13). "If Timothy comes, see that he is with you without fear....Send him forward in peace that he may come to me....And concerning our brother Apollos, I *urged* him many times to come to you" (1 Cor. 16:10-12). "We *entreated* Titus" (2 Cor. 8:6). "Titus...received the *entreaty*....And we *sent* together with him the brother" (2 Cor. 8:16-18). "We *sent* with them our brother" (2 Cor. 8:22). "Tychicus, the beloved brother...I have *sent* to you" (Eph. 6:21-22). "But I considered it necessary to *send* to you Epaphroditus" (Phil. 2:25). "All the things concerning me, Tychicus...will make known to you" (Col. 4:7). "Luke, the beloved physician, greets you, as well as Demas" (Col. 4:14). "And *say to* Archippus, Take heed to the ministry" (Col. 4:17). "We *sent* Timothy" (1 Thes. 3:1-2). "*Be diligent* to come to me quickly....Take Mark and *bring* him with you....But Tychicus I have *sent* to Ephesus" (2 Tim. 4:9-12). "Trophimus I *left* at Miletus sick. *Be diligent* to come before winter" (2 Tim. 4:20-21). "For this cause *I left* you in Crete, that you might set in order the things which I have begun that remain and appoint elders in every city, as *I directed you*" (Titus 1:5). "When I *send* Artemas to you or Tychicus, *be diligent* to come to me at Nicopolis, for I have decided to spend the winter there. Zenas the lawyer and Apollos *send forward diligently* that nothing may be lacking to them" (Titus 3:12-13).

The above Scriptures show us that among the workers of God dependence upon Him does not render us independent of one another. We saw that Paul *left* Titus in Crete to complete the work he himself had left unfinished, and that he afterwards *sent* Artemas and Tychicus to replace him when he instructed him to proceed to Nicopolis. On various occasions he appointed Timothy and Tychicus to do certain work, and we read that he *persuaded* Titus and Apollos to remain in Corinth. We observe that these workers not only learned to work in teams, but the less experienced learned to submit to the direction of the more spiritual. God's workers must learn to be left, to be sent, and to be persuaded.

It is important to recognize the difference between official and spiritual authority. In an organization all authority is official, not spiritual. In a good organization the one who holds office has both official and spiritual authority; in a bad organization the authority wielded is only official. But in any organization, no matter whether the office-bearer *himself* has spiritual authority or not, the authority he holds in the organization is actually only official. What is the meaning of official authority? It means that because a man holds office, therefore, he exercises authority. The authority is exercised solely on account of the office he holds. As long as the office-bearer retains his position, just so long can he exert his authority; as soon as he resigns office, his authority ceases. Such authority is altogether objective; it is not inherent in the man himself. It is connected not with the person, but merely with his position. If he holds the office of superintendent, it follows as a matter of course that he superintends affairs, no matter whether he is spiritually qualified to do so or not. If he holds the office of director, then automatically he directs, even if lack of spirituality should really disqualify him from exercising control over other lives. The life of an organization is position; it is position that determines authority.

But in divinely constituted companies of workers there is no organization. Authority *is* exercised among them, but such authority is spiritual, not official. It is an authority based upon spirituality, an authority which is the outcome of a deep knowledge of the Lord, and intimate fellowship with Him. Spiritual life is the source of such authority. The reason Paul could direct others was not because of his superior position, but because of his greater spirituality. If he had lost his spirituality, he would have lost his authority. In an organization those who are spiritual do not necessarily hold any office, and those who hold office are not necessarily spiritual; but in Scripture it is otherwise. There it is those who know the Lord who superintend affairs. It is those who are spiritual that direct others, and if those others are spiritual, they will recognize spiritual authority and will submit to it. In an organization its workers are obliged to obey, but in a spiritual association they are not, and from an official point of view no fault can be found with them if they do not obey. In a spiritual association there is no compulsion; direction and submission alike are on the ground of spirituality.

Apart from the question of spiritual authority there is also the question of different ministries. All servants of the Lord are in the ministry, and each has his own special ministry. In an organization, positions are allotted by man, but in spiritual work ministries are appointed by the Lord. Because of difference of ministry, we must on the one hand obey the Lord, and on the other we must obey the brethren. Such obedience is not on the ground of their superior position, but because their ministry differs from ours, and yet both are intimately related. If the head is moving the tips of my fingers, the muscles of my arms cannot take an independent attitude and refuse to move with them. The principle of being in one Body necessitates the closely related members to move with one another. In moving with the other members, we are not really obeying them; we are obeying the Head. In many things we can claim a direct guidance from the Head, but in just as many things the Head moves others and we simply *move with them*. Their movement is reason enough for us to fall in. It is most important to recognize this relatedness of various ministries in the Body of Christ. We have to know our ministry and to recognize the ministry of others, so that we can move as one obeying those who have a greater ministry. Since our ministry is interrelated in such a way, we dare not take an individual or independent attitude.

All positions held by God's ministers are spiritual, not official. Alas! men have only seen half the truth, so they try to organize the work and appoint a director to supcrintend the service of others, but their directing is based upon their position in the organization, not upon their position in the ministry. The reason Paul could direct others was that the ministry committed to him by the Lord put him in a position of authority over them; and the reason Titus, Timothy, and Tychicus could submit to being directed was that the ministry committed to them by the Lord put them in a position under his authority. Unfortunately, the directing of today is based upon neither depth of spirituality nor greatness of ministry.

Timothy was a man of God. He lived close to the Lord, obeying and serving Him faithfully; yet many a time he was sent here or there by Paul. He did not say, Do you think I am incapable of working by myself? Do you think I do not know how to preach the gospel and how to found churches? Do you think I do not know how to go about things? Although Timothy knew a lot, he was willing to obey Paul. In spiritual work there is such a thing as being directed by others; there is the position of a Paul, and there is also the position of a Timothy, but these are spiritual, not official, positions.

Today we must learn on the one hand to maintain a right relationship with our fellow workers, and on the other hand to be guided by the Holy Spirit. We must maintain both relationships and also maintain the balance between the two. In the first and second Epistles to Timothy there are many passages which illustrate how fellow workers should cooperate, and how a younger worker should submit to an older one. A young Timothy ought to obey the commands of the Holy Spirit, but he ought also to receive the instructions of an elderly Paul. Timothy was sent out by Paul, Timothy was left by Paul at Ephesus, and Timothy obeyed Paul in the Lord. Here is an example for young servants of God. It is most important in His work to learn how to be led by the Spirit and how, at the same time, to cooperate with our fellow workers. The responsibility must not be wholly upon Timothy; neither must it rest wholly upon Paul. In the work Timothy must learn to fit in with Paul, and Paul must also learn to fit in with Timothy. Not only must the younger learn to submit to the instructions of the elder, but the elder must learn how to instruct the younger. The one who is in a position to leave, send, or persuade must learn not to follow the dictates of his own nature, acting according to personal inclination or desire, for in that case he will make it difficult for those under his authority. Paul must direct Timothy in such a way that he will not find it hard to obey both the Holy Spirit and the apostle.

God's servants must work together in companies, but there is a kind of co-working which is to be avoided, that is, co-working in a man-made organization which restricts its members so that they cannot really respond to the leading of the Spirit. When workers are entirely subject to the direction of men, then their work is not the outcome of a spiritual burden placed on them by God, but merely the doing of a piece of work in response to the dictates of those holding higher positions than they. The trouble today is that men are taking the place of the Holy Spirit, and the will of men in official position is taking the place of the will of God. Workers have no direct knowledge of the divine will, but simply do the will of those in authority over them, without bearing any personal burden from the Lord for His work.

There are others again who know the mind of God, have a call from Him, and depend entirely upon Him for the meeting of all their needs; but while they know what it is to be led of Him individually, they fancy they can just go their own way and do their own work in independence of others.

The teaching of God's Word is that, on the one hand, human organizations must not control the servants of God; on the other hand, His servants must learn to submit to a *spiritual* authority which is based on the difference of ministry. There is no organized cooperation, yet there is a spiritual fellowship and a spiritual oneness. Individualism and human organization alike are out of line with the will of God. We should seek to know His will, not independently, but in conjunction with the other ministering members of the Body. The call of Paul and Barnabas was on this principle. It was not a case of two prophets and teachers only, but of five, waiting upon God to know His will. Acts 13 gives us a good example of a working company, all the workers being mutually related, and the guidance of one confirmed by the others.

THE SPHERE OF THE WORK

The sphere of the work, unlike the sphere of the local church, is very wide. Some of the workers are sent to Ephesus, some go to Paul at Nicopolis, some stay on in Corinth, some are left in Miletus, some remain in Crete, some return to Thessalonica, and others go on to Galatia. Such is the work! We see here not the movements of the local church but of the work, for the movements of the local church are always confined to one locality. Ephesus only manages the affairs of Ephesus, and Rome the affairs of Rome. The church confines herself to matters in her own locality. There is no need for the church in Ephesus to send a man to Corinth, or for the church in Corinth to leave a man in Rome. The church here is local, the work extra-local. Ephesus, Corinth, and Rome are all the concern of the workers. The church only manages the affairs in any given locality, but the workers of God regard as their "parish" the sphere which *the Lord has measured out* to them.

NO CENTRAL CONTROL, BUT FELLOWSHIP

In Scripture the workers were formed into companies, but that does not imply that *all* the apostles formed themselves into *one* company and placed everything under one *central control*. Although Paul had "those with him," and Peter his associates, they comprised only a number of apostles, not all the apostles. That all the apostles should combine into one company is not shown in the Word of God. It is quite in order for scores of men, or even hundreds, who have received the same trust from God, to join together in the same work; but in the Scriptures we find no centralization of authority for the control of *all* the apostles. There is a company of apostles, but it is not great enough to include *all* the apostles. That is Romish, not scriptural.

The parties referred to in Philippians 1:15-17, 2 Corinthians 11:12-13, 22-23, and Galatians 4:17 all indicate that the work in the early days was not centralized. Had it been centralized, those groups could not have remained in existence, for they could have been dealt with effectively. The

Scriptures show that in divine work there is no universal organization or central control, which accounts for the fact that the apostle had no authority to deal with those groups of people who were creating such difficulty in the churches. The explanation is this: God does not wish the power of organization to take the place of the power of the Holy Spirit. Even though there is no central control, provided all the workers follow the leading of the Spirit, everything will run smoothly and satisfactorily, and there will be the coordination of a body. Whenever people cease to obey the Spirit and labor in the power of the flesh, then it is best if the work is simply allowed to fall to pieces. A good organization often serves as a bad substitute for the power of the Holy Spirit, by holding a work together even after all its vitality is gone. When life has departed from the work and the scaffolding of organization still supports it, its collapse is prevented; but that is doubtful gain, for a splendid outward organization may be blinding God's servants to a deep inward need. God would rather His work be discontinued than that it go on with such a counterfeit for spiritual power. When the glory of God had departed from the temple, He himself left it to utter ruin. God desires that the outward and inward conditions should correspond, so that if death invades a work, His workers may awaken at once to their need and in humility of heart seek His face.

Central control has many evils. It makes it easy for God's servants to disregard the leading of the Spirit, and readily develops into a popish system, becoming a great worldly power. It is a scriptural fact that God's servants are formed into companies, but they are not formed into one single company.

However, that does not mean that every company could just go on independently, knowing no relatedness or fellowship with other companies. The principle of the oneness of the Body holds good here as in all other relationships between the children of God. In Scripture we not only see the principle of "the laying on of hands," but also that of giving "the right hand" (Gal. 2:9). The former speaks of *identification;* the latter of *fellowship*. In Antioch hands were laid on Paul and

Barnabas; in Jerusalem there was no laying on of hands, but the right hand of fellowship given them by James, Cephas, and John. In Antioch the sphere in view was *one* apostolic company, and the point *emphasized* was identification; consequently, hands were laid on them. But in Jerusalem the sphere in view was the relationship between *different* apostolic companies, and the point emphasized was fellowship; consequently, the right hand was extended to them.

Many are called to work for the Lord, but their sphere of service is not the same, so it follows that their associates cannot be the same. But the various companies must all be identified with the Body, coming under the headship of the Lord, and having fellowship among themselves. There is no laying on of hands between Antioch and Jerusalem, but there is the giving of the right hand of fellowship. So the Word of God does not warrant the forming of one central company; neither does it warrant the forming of various scattered, unrelated, and isolated companies. There is no one central place for the laying on of hands, nor is there *merely* the laying on of hands and nothing else in any one of the various groups; but among them there is also the giving of the right hand of fellowship one to the other. Each company should recognize what God is doing with the other companies and should extend fellowship to them, acknowledging that they are also ministers in the Body. Under the ordering of God they may work in different companies, but all must work as one Body. The extending of the right hand of fellowship implies a recognition that other people are in the Body and we are in fellowship with them, working together in a related way, as becomes functioning members of the same Body. "Seeing that I had been entrusted with the gospel to the uncircumcision...and perceiving the grace given to me, James and Cephas and John, who were reputed to be pillars, gave to me and to Barnabas the right hand of fellowship that we should go to the Gentiles, and they, to the circumcision" (Gal. 2:7-9). The unrelated, scattered, disrupted, and conflicting organizations in Christendom, which do not recognize the principle of the Body and do not come under the sovereignty and headship of Christ, are never according to the mind of the Lord.

COOPERATION AMONG THE WORKERS

The question naturally arises, how should workers and working associations cooperate? To one company God gives one kind of ministry, and to another an altogether different form of ministry. How should the various groups work together? Peter and his associates, and Paul and those with him, were appointed to different spheres, but in the event of their work overlapping, how should they act? Since there is no centralization of work, yet at the same time there are various groups of workers, how should these different groups cooperate? We must note two fundamental points in regard to the work:

(1) The first responsibility of every worker—no matter what his ministry or what his special line of work—whenever he comes to a place where there is no *local* church, is to establish one in the locality. (What applies to the individual worker applies also to any group of workers.)

(2) Should he come to a place where a local church already exists, then all his teaching and all his experience must be contributed to that church, that it may be strengthened and edified, and no attempt should be made to attach that church to himself or to the society he represents.

If a worker goes to a place where there is no church and founds one there for the propagation of his particular doctrine, then we cannot cooperate with him because he is building up a sect, and not a church. On the other hand, should a worker go to a place where there is already a local church, and instead of contributing his teaching and experience to its upbuilding, seek to make it a branch-church of the society to which he belongs, then again it is impossible for us to cooperate, because he is building up a denomination. The basis of fellowship in the church is the common possession of life in Christ and living in the same locality. *The basis of cooperation in the work is the common aim of the founding and building up of local churches.* Denominational affiliations do not hinder us from reckoning anyone as belonging to the Body, but the aim of denominational extension will certainly keep us from any cooperation in the service of God. The greatest harm a worker can do is, instead of establishing and edifying the local churches, to attach to his society the believers he finds in a place, or to form those brought to the Lord through his labors into a branch of his particular denomination. Both these procedures are condemned by the Word of God.

Paul came from Antioch to Corinth and there he preached the gospel. People believed and were saved, and soon there was a group of saints in Corinth. Into what kind of church did Paul form them? Into the church in Corinth. Paul did not establish an Anitochian church in Corinth. He did not form a branch-church of Antioch in Corinth, but simply established a church in Corinth. Thereafter Peter came to Corinth and preached the gospel, with the result that another group of people believed. Did Peter say, "Paul came from Antioch, but I am come from Jerusalem, so I must set up another church: I will establish a Jerusalemic church in Corinth, or, I will form a branch-church of Jerusalem here in Corinth"? No, he contributed all those he led to the Lord to the already existing local church in Corinth. After a while Apollos came along. Again people were saved, and again all the saved ones were added to the local church. So in Corinth there was only one church of God; there were no schismatic denominations. Had Paul established the precedent of founding a church in Corinth to enlarge the sphere of the church from which he went out, calling it the Antiochian church in Corinth, then when Peter came to Corinth he might well have argued, "It is all right for Paul to found an Antiochian church in Corinth since *he* came from Antioch, but I have nothing to do with Antioch; *my* church is in Jerusalem, so I must establish a Jerusalemic church here." Apollos coming to Corinth would in turn follow their example and establish another church as a branch of the one from which *he* came out. If every worker tried to form a branch of the church he represented, then sects and denominations would be utterly inevitable. If the aim of a worker in any place is not to establish a local church there, but to enlarge the church from which he has gone out, then he is not establishing a church of God in that locality, but only building up his own society. Under such circumstances there is *no possibility of cooperation.*

Conditions have greatly changed since the days of the early apostles. Christianity has lost its original purity, and everything connected with it is in a false and confused state. Despite that fact, our work today is still the same as in the days of the early apostles—to found and build up local churches, the local expressions of the Body of Christ. So if we are in a place where there is no church, we should seek the Lord's face that He may enable us to win souls for Himself and form them into a local church. If we are in a place where there are missions, or churches, standing on sectarian or denominational ground, but no church standing on the ground of the Body and the locality, then our duty is just the same, that is, to found and build a local church. Many will still persist in their old ways; hence, the persons standing on clear church ground may be far fewer than the total number of Christians in the locality. But the area of the ground on which they stand is just as wide as that on which the church ought to stand, so it is still our duty to maintain that ground. We can only cooperate with those who are building up the Body of Christ as expressed in local churches, and not with those who are building up something else. Denominational connection does not hinder us from fellowship in the Lord, but denominational extension does hinder us from cooperation in the work of God.

Here is the most important principle in the work of God—a worker must not seek to establish a branch of the church from which he goes out, but to establish a church in the locality to which he comes. He does not make the church in the place to which he goes to be an extension of the church in the place from which he comes, but he founds a church in that locality. Wherever he goes, he establishes a church in *that* place. He does not extend the church of his place of origin, but establishes the church in the place of his adoption. Since in Scripture all churches are local, Jerusalem and Antioch can have no branch-churches. We cannot extend one local church to another locality; we can only form a *new* church in that locality. The church which the apostles established in

Ephesus is the church in Ephesus; the church which they established in Philippi is the church in Philippi; the churches which they established in other places are the churches of those different places. There is no precedent in Scripture for establishing any other than local churches. It is all right to extend *the* Church of God, but it is all wrong to extend *a* local church of God. What is the place in which I intend to work? It is the church in *that* place I must seek to establish.

Now there are two kinds of workers, namely, those who stand on scriptural ground, and those who stand on denominational or mission ground. But even with those who stand on denominational or mission ground, the principle of cooperation is just the same—the one aim of founding and building up the local church.

The work of evangelization is primarily for the salvation of sinners, but its spontaneous result is a church in the place where such work is done. The immediate object is the salvation of men, but the ultimate result is the formation of churches. The danger which confronts the missionary is to form those he has led to the Lord into a branch of the society he represents. Since workers represent different societies, they naturally form different branches of their respective societies, and the consequence is great confusion in the work and churches of God. The immediate aim of the various workers is no doubt the same—what preacher does not hope that many souls will be won to the Lord?—but there is a lack of clarity and definiteness regarding the ultimate issue. Some workers, praise God, are out to establish local churches; others, alas! are out to extend their own denomination or to form mission churches.

This is a point on which my fellow workers and I cannot see eye to eye with many of God's children. From the depths of our hearts we thank God that in the past century He has sent so many of His faithful servants to China, so that those who were sitting in darkness should hear the gospel and believe in the Lord. Their self-sacrifice, their diligence, and their godliness have truly been an example to us. Many a time, as we looked at the faces of missionaries suffering for the gospel's sake, we have been moved to pray, "Lord, make us to live like them." May God bless and reward them! We acknowledge that we are utterly unworthy to have any part in the work of God, but by the grace of God we are what we are, and since God in His grace has called us to His service, we cannot but seek to be faithful. We have nothing to criticize, and much to admire, as far as the gospel work of our missionary brethren is concerned; yet we cannot but question their methods in dealing with the fruits of such work. For in the past hundred years it has not resulted in the building up of local churches but in the forming of missionary churches, or of branch churches of the various denominations which the missionaries represented. In our opinion this is contrary to the Word of God. There is no such thing in Scripture as the building up of denominations; we only find local churches there. May God forgive me if I am wrong!

LOCAL CHURCHES AND MISSION CHURCHES

Permit me to mention a personal incident. Some time ago I met a certain missionary in Shanghai who asked me if it would not be possible for me to cooperate with his mission. Not knowing quite what to say, I did not commit myself. Later on I came across him in another part of the country, and again he repeated his question and asked if I had anything against the mission. I answered, "I dare not criticize your mission, though I do not believe it is according to the full thought of God. I believe it was God's will to establish it so that the servants of God in Western lands could come to China to preach the gospel. I have nothing to say regarding the mission as a body, for the Scriptures speak of companies of workers, and if you feel it should be organized, should have officers, and should bear a specific name, you must answer to God and not to man for that. Who am I that I should criticize the servants of the Lord? But while I do not criticize, I cannot copy, because God has not revealed that as His will and way for me. Regarding the mission as a mission, I have nothing to say, but I have serious questions regarding the churches formed by the mission. To illustrate, you represent the 'X' Mission. Now, do those saved by your instrumentality become the 'X' Church, or do they become the church of the particular locality in which they live? It may be all right for missionaries to belong to the 'X' Mission, but it is all wrong for them to form the fruits of the mission into the 'X' Church. The Word of God has not definitely forbidden the forming of an 'X' Mission, but it clearly does not sanction the founding of other than local churches."

Then I mentioned the apostolic examples, pointing out that they always sought to found or build up churches in the locality of their labors with the fruit of such labors. They never used such fruit to form branches of the companies in which they worked; otherwise, the Church of God would have been rent by numerous factions from its very inception.

I then took as an illustration the work at T——. "There at T——," I said, "God has used you to win many souls. If the people saved by your instrumentality are the church in T——, then if I come to T—— I shall certainly join them, no matter what their spiritual state, or what their form of organization; otherwise, I should be guilty of sectarianism. But if you build up an 'X' Church in T—— with the people saved there, then you are not building the Church of God in T——, and such a 'church' I regret to say I cannot join. I shall be obliged to work separately in T—— unless there is a church there standing on the scriptural ground of locality.

"If we are all out to establish local churches, then there is every possibility of cooperation. It is permissible to establish an 'X' Mission, but it is not scriptural to establish an 'X' Church. Suppose your 'X' Mission coming to T—— establishes an 'X' Church; thereafter, various other missions come to T——, each establishing a separate mission 'church.' That would be the same as Paul establishing an Antiochian church in Corinth, and Peter coming along shortly after and establishing a Jerusalemic church there. On such a basis cooperation is impossible, for we should be disregarding the pattern which God has clearly shown us in His Word—the establishment of local churches.

"If we come to a place to found a church, then it must be local, intensely local, without anything extraneous to rob it in the slightest of its local character. If you come to T—— with the establishing of the church in T—— as your one aim, and I come to T—— with the establishing of the church in T—— as my one aim, then cooperation will be no problem. Even if a hundred and one missionaries, representing a hundred and one missions, all come to T—— with this as their one aim, to establish the church in T——, then there will be no possibility of sectarianism, and cooperation will be a matter of course. If the aim of the 'X' Mission is only to preach the gospel, then it is possible for us to work together; but if there is a twofold aim—the preaching of the gospel and the extension of the mission—then cooperation is not possible. If a worker seeks on the one hand to preach the gospel, and on the other hand to extend his own society, it is impossible for us to work together." Whether or not a man is out to establish local churches determines whether or not we can cooperate with him. No matter to what mission a man may belong, if he comes to a place not seeking to establish his own "church," but a church in the locality, then we are perfectly willing to work with him. Although we are not a mission, we are quite prepared to cooperate with any mission if they have no private end in view, but only the one end which God has shown as His will regarding His work.

May God grant us grace to see that His churches are all local churches.

Chapter Eight

THE QUESTION OF FINANCE

It is a remarkable fact that, while the book of Acts supplies many minute details regarding the work of an apostle, the one subject which from a human standpoint is of paramount importance in the carrying on of any work is not dealt with at all. No information whatever is given as to how the needs of the work or the personal needs of the workers were supplied. This is certainly amazing! What men consider of supreme importance, the apostles regarded of least consequence. In the early days of the Church, God's sent ones went out under the constraint of divine love. Their work was not just their profession, and their faith in God was not intellectual, but spiritual; not just theoretical, but intensely practical. The love and the faithfulness of God were realities to them, and that being so, no question arose in their minds concerning the supply of their temporal needs. Today as then, the matter of finance will present no problems to those who have a vital faith in God and a real love for Him.

This question of finance has most important issues, so let us devote a little time to it. In grace God is the greatest power, but in the world mammon is the greatest. If God's servants do not clearly settle the question of finance, then they leave a vast number of other questions unsettled too. Once the financial problem is solved, it is amazing how many other problems are automatically solved with it. The attitude of Christian workers to financial matters will be a fairly good indication as to whether or not they have been commissioned of God. If the work is of God, it will be spiritual; and if the work is spiritual, the way of supply will be spiritual. If supplies are not on a spiritual plane, then the work itself will speedily drift on to the plane of secular business. If spirituality does not characterize the financial side of the work, then the spirituality of its other departments is merely theoretical. There is no feature of the work that touches practical issues as truly as its finance. You can be theoretical in any other department, but not in that one.

THE IMPORTANCE OF THE LIFE OF FAITH

Every worker, no matter what his ministry, must exercise faith for the meeting of all his personal needs and all the needs of his work. In God's Word we read of no worker asking for, or receiving, a salary for his services. Paul made no contract with the church in Ephesus, or with any other church, that he should receive a certain remuneration for a certain period of service. That God's servants should look to human sources for the supply of their needs has no precedent in Scripture. We do read there of a Balaam who sought to make merchandise of his gift of prophecy, but he is denounced in no uncertain terms. We read also of a Gehazi who sought to make gain of the grace of God, but he was stricken with leprosy for his sin. No servant of God should look to any human agency, whether an individual or a society, for the meeting of his temporal needs. If they can be met by the labor of his own hands, or from a private income, *well and good*. Otherwise, he should be directly dependent on God alone for their supply, as were the early apostles. The twelve apostles sent out by the Lord had no fixed salary, nor had any of the apostles sent out by the Spirit; they simply looked to the Lord to meet all their requirements. The apostles of today, like those of the early days, should regard no man as their employer, but should trust Him who has sent them forth to bear the responsibility of all that the doing of His will involves, in temporal as well as spiritual matters.

If a man can trust God, let him go out and work for Him; if not, let him stay at home, for he lacks the first qualification for the work. There is an idea prevalent that if a worker has a settled income he can be more at leisure for the work, and consequently will do it better; but as a matter of fact, in spiritual work there is need for an unsettled income, because that necessitates intimate fellowship with God, constant clear revelation of His will, and direct divine support. In worldly business, all a worker needs by way of equipment is will and talent; but human zeal and natural gift are no equipment for spiritual service. Utter dependence on God is necessary if the work is to be according to His will; therefore, God wishes His workers to be *cast on* Him alone for financial supplies, so that they cannot but walk in close communion with Him and learn to trust Him continually. A settled income does not foster trust in God and fellowship with Him; but utter dependence on Him for the meeting of one's needs certainly does. The more unsettled a worker's living is, the more he will be cast on God; and the more an attitude of trustful dependence on God is cultivated, the more spiritual the work will be. So it is clear that the nature of the work and the source of its supply are closely related. If a worker receives a definite salary from man, the work produced can never be purely divine.

Faith is a most important factor in God's service, for without it there can be no truly spiritual work; but our faith requires training and strengthening, and material needs are a means used in God's hand toward that end. We may profess to have faith in God for a vast variety of intangible things, and we may deceive ourselves into believing we really trust Him when we have no trust at all, simply because there is nothing concrete to demonstrate our distrust. But when it comes to financial needs, the matter is so practical that the reality of our faith is put to the test at once. If we cannot trust God to supply our temporal needs, then we cannot trust Him to supply our spiritual needs; but if we truly prove His trustworthiness in the very practical realm of material wants, we shall be able also to trust Him when spiritual difficulties arise either in connection with the work or with our personal lives. What a contradiction it is if we proclaim to others that God is the living God, yet we ourselves dare not trust Him for the meeting of our material needs.

Further, he who holds the purse holds authority. If we are supported by men, our work will be controlled by men. It is only to be expected that if we receive an income from a certain source, we should have to account for our doings to such a source. Whenever our trust is in men, our work cannot but be influenced by men. It is a serious misconception to fancy that we can take money from men to do the work of God. If we are supported by men, then we must seek to please men, and it is often impossible at the same time both to please men and God.

In His own work God must have the sole direction. That is why He wishes us to depend on no human source for financial supplies. Many of us have experienced that again and again God has controlled us through money matters. When we have been in the center of His will, supplies have been sure, but as soon as we have been out of vital touch with Him, they have been uncertain. At times we have fancied God would have us do a certain thing, but He has showed us it was not His will by withholding financial supplies. So we have been under the constant direction of the Lord, and such direction is most precious. If we cease to be dependent on Him, how can our trust be developed?

The first question anyone should face who believes himself truly called of God is the financial question. If he cannot look to the Lord alone for the meeting of his daily wants, then he is not qualified to be engaged in His work, for if he is not financially independent of men, the work cannot be independent of men either. If he cannot trust God for the supply of needed funds, can he trust Him in all the problems and difficulties of the work? If we are utterly dependent on God for our supplies, then we are responsible to Him alone for our work, and in that case it need not come under human direction. May I advise all who are not prepared for the walk of faith, to continue with their secular duties and not engage in spiritual service. Every worker for God must be able to trust Him.

If we have real faith in God, then we have to bear all the responsibility of our own needs and the needs of the work. We must not secretly hope for help from some human source. We must have faith in God alone, not in God plus man. If the brethren show their love, let us thank God, but if they do not, let us thank Him still. It is a shameful thing for a servant of God to have one eye on Him and one eye on man or circumstance. It is unworthy of any Christian worker to profess to trust in God and yet hope for help from other sources. This is sheer unbelief. I have constantly said, and say it again, that as soon as our eyes turn to the brethren, we bring disgrace on our fellow workers and on the name of the Lord. Our living by faith must be absolutely real, and not deteriorate into a "living by charity." We dare to be utterly independent of men in financial matters, because we dare to believe utterly in God; we dare to cast away all hope in them, because we have full confidence in Him.

If our hope is in men, then when their resources dry up, ours will dry up too. We have no board behind us, but we have a Rock beneath us; and no one standing on this Rock will ever be put to shame. Men and circumstances may change, but we shall carry on in a steady course if our reliance is on God. All the silver and the gold are His, and none who walk in His will can ever come to want. We are apt to trust in the children of the Lord who in bygone days have sent us gifts, but they will all pass away. We must keep our eyes fixed on the unchanging God whose grace and faithfulness continue forever.

The two initial steps in the work of God are—first, the prayer of faith for needed funds, then the actual undertaking of the work. Today, alas! many of God's servants have no faith; yet they seek to serve Him. They undertake the work without having the essential qualification for it; therefore, what they do has no spiritual value. Faith is the first essential in any work for God, and it should be exercised in relation to material as well as other needs. If there is no faith for funds, then no matter how good the work is, sooner or later it will fail. When money stops, the work will stop too.

LIVING FROM THE GOSPEL

Our Lord said, "The worker is worthy of his wages" (Luke 10:7); and Paul wrote to the Corinthians, "So also the Lord directed those who announce the gospel to live from the gospel" (1 Cor. 9:14). What is the meaning of living from the gospel? It does not mean that God's servant should receive a definite allowance from the church, for the modern system of paid service in the work of God was unknown in Paul's day. What it does mean is that the preachers of the gospel *may receive gifts* from the brethren; but no stipulations are made in connection with such gifts. No definite period of time is named, no definite sum of money, and no definite responsibility; all is a matter of freewill. As the hearts of believers are touched by God, they give gifts to His servants, so that while these servants receive gifts *through* men, their trust is still entirely in God. It is upon *Him* their eyes are fixed, it is to *Him* their needs are told, and it is He who touches the hearts of *His* children to give. That is what Paul meant when he spoke of living from the gospel. Paul himself received the gift from the church in Philippi (Phil. 4:16), and when he was in Corinth, he was helped by the brothers in Macedonia (2 Cor. 11:9). These are examples of living from the gospel. Paul received occasional gifts from individuals and from churches, but he received no definite remuneration for his preaching.

Yes, "the worker is worthy of his wages," and he should certainly live from the gospel. But we do well to ask ourselves, Whose laborers are we? If we are the laborers of men, then let us look to men for our support; but if we are the laborers of God, then we must look to no other but Him, though He may meet our needs through our fellow men. The whole question hinges here: Has God called us and sent us out? If the call and the commission have come from Him, then He must and surely will be responsible for all that our obedience to Him involves. When we make our needs known to Him, He will certainly hear, and He will move the hearts of men to supply us with all we need. If we are only volunteers in God's service, then God will not be responsible for the liabilities we incur, so we shall be unable to live from the gospel.

When Miss M. E. Barber thought of coming to China to serve the Lord, she foresaw the difficulties of a woman setting out on her own for a foreign country, so she asked advice of Mr. Wilkinson of the Mildmay Mission to the Jews, who said, "A foreign country, no promise of support, no backing of any society—all these present no problem. The question is here: Are you going on your own initiative, or are you being sent by God?" "God is sending me," she replied. "Then no more questions are necessary," he said, "for if *God* sends you, *He* must be responsible." Yes, if we go on our own initiative, then distress and shame await us, but if we go as sent ones of God, all responsibility will be His, and we need never inquire how He is going to discharge it.

But in Corinth Paul did not live from the gospel; he made tents with his own hands. So there are evidently two ways by which the needs of God's servants may be met—either they look to God to touch the hearts of His children to give what is needful, or they earn it by doing part-time secular work. To work with our hands may be very good, but we need to note that Paul does not regard that as the usual thing. It is something exceptional, a course to be resorted to in special circumstances.

"If we have sown to you the spiritual things, is it a great thing if we shall reap from you the fleshly things? If others partake of this right over you, should not rather we? Yet we did not use this right, but we bear all things that we may not cause any hindrance to the gospel of Christ. Do you not know that those who labor on the sacred things eat the things of the sacred temple, that those who attend to the altar have their portion with the altar? So also the Lord directed those who announce the gospel to live from the gospel. But I myself have not used any of these things; and I have not written these things that it may be so with me; for it is good for me rather to die than—No one shall make my boast void.... What then is my reward? That in preaching the gospel I may present the gospel without charge, so as not to use to the full my right in the gospel" (1 Cor. 9:11-15, 18). There are certain rights which are the privilege of all preachers of the gospel. Paul did not receive anything from Corinth, because he was in special circumstances at the time; but though he did not avail himself of his privileges as a gospel preacher on that occasion, that he did so at other times is quite clear. "Or did I commit a sin, abasing myself that you might be exalted, because I announced the gospel of God to you free of charge? I robbed other churches, taking wages for the ministry to you. And when I was present with you and lacked, I was not a burden to anyone; for the brothers who came from Macedonia filled up my lack, and in everything I kept myself from being burdensome to you, and will keep myself. The truthfulness of Christ is in me, that this boasting shall not be stopped as it regards me in the regions of Achaia" (2 Cor. 11:7-10).

THE PRINCIPLE OF RECEIVING GIFTS

It is not permissible to receive a definite salary from a church, and at times it is not even permissible to receive an indefinite gift. Paul was demonstrating this principle in not receiving anything from the Corinthian church. If anyone gives us a gift out of pity for us, then for the Lord's sake we dare not accept it; or if gifts are offered, the reception of which would either bring us under obligation to the givers, or bring us under their control, we must refuse them too. All the servants of God must not only trust Him entirely for the supply of their needs, but when gifts are freely offered them, they must be able to discern clearly whether or not such gifts could be received by God.

In the Old Testament the tithes of the Israelites were handed over to the Levites. The Israelites made their offerings to God, not to the Levites, but the latter stood in the place of God to receive the offerings. Today we are standing in the position of the Levites, and the gifts that are proffered to us are really offered to God. We do not receive gifts from any man; therefore, we are under obligation to none. If anyone wants thanks, he must seek it from God, for God is the One who receives the offerings. Therefore, whenever a gift is given to us, it is essential for us to be clear whether or not God could receive that gift. If God could not receive it, neither dare we. We dare not accept gifts indiscriminately lest we put God into a false position. (I say this reverently.) There are many people whose lives are not well-pleasing to God; how then could God receive their offerings? If He cannot, then we dare not do so in His stead. We should only receive money when our doing so involves no obligation on our part, and on God's part no misrepresentation of His nature.

It may happen at times that the gift is right, and also the attitude of the giver; but on the strength of his gift the giver may consider himself entitled to a say in the work. It is quite in order for the offerer to specify in what direction his offering be used, but it is not in order for him to decide how the work should be done. No servant of God should sacrifice his liberty to follow the divine leading by accepting any money which puts him under human control. A giver is at perfect liberty to stipulate to what use his gift should be put, but as soon as it is given, he should take hands off, and not seek to utilize it as a means of exercising indirect control over the work. If he can trust a servant of God, let him trust him; if not, then he need not give his money to him.

In secular work the man who supplies the means exercises authority in the realm to which his means are devoted, but not so in spiritual work. All authority in the work rests with the *one who has been called of God to do it*. In the spiritual realm it is the worker who controls the money, not the money the worker. The one to whom the call has come, and to whom the work has been entrusted by God, is the one to whom God will reveal the way the work must be carried out, and he dare not receive money from anyone who would use his gift to interfere with the Lord's will as it is revealed to him concerning the work. If a giver is *spiritual,* we shall gladly seek his counsel, but his advice can be sought *solely on the ground of his spirituality, not on the ground of his gift.* If he can trust us, and if he is clear the Lord is leading him to give it to us, then we may receive his offering; otherwise, let him keep his money, and let us go on with God's work in the way He has directed, looking to Him alone to supply its needs and ours.

In all our service for God we must maintain an attitude of utter dependence on Him. Whether funds are abundant or low, let us steadfastly pursue our work, recognizing it as a trust committed to us by God, and a matter for which we must answer to Him alone. "Am I seeking to please men? If I were still trying to please men, I would not be a slave of Christ" (Gal. 1:10). We must remain absolutely independent of men as regards the financial side of the work, but even in our independence we must preserve an attitude of true humility and willingness to accept advice from every member of the Body who is in close contact with the Head; and we should expect through them confirmation of the leading we have received direct from God. But all the counsel we seek and receive from others is on account of their spirituality, not on account of their financial position. We are willing to seek advice of the richest member of the Body, neither because of nor despite his money, and we are just as ready to seek the counsel of the poorest member, neither because of nor despite his poverty. In matters of finance we must maintain this ground, that it is God alone we have to do with. Let Paul's boasting be ours too!

ATTITUDE TOWARD THE GENTILES

The principle is "taking nothing from the Gentiles" (3 John 7). We dare not receive any support for the work of God from those who do not know Him. If God has not accepted a man, He can never accept his money, and only what God can accept dare His servants accept. If anyone engaged in God's service accepts money for the furtherance of the work from an unsaved man, then he virtually places God under obligation to sinners. Let us never receive money on God's behalf which would enable a sinner before the great white throne to charge God with having taken advantage of him. However, this does not mean that we need reject even the hospitality of the Gentiles. If in the providence of God we visit some Miletus, then we should do well to accept the hospitality of a friendly Publius. But this must be definitely under the ordering of God, not as a matter of regular occurrence. Our principle should always be to take nothing from the Gentiles. When we begin to use their money, our work will have fallen into a sorry state.

THE CHURCHES AND THE WORKERS

Should the churches provide for the needs of the workers? God's Word supplies a clear answer to our question. We see there that the money collected by the churches is used in three different ways:

(1) For the poor saints. The Scriptures pay much attention to the needy children of God, and a large proportion of the local offerings goes to relieve their distress.

(2) For the elders of the local church. Circumstances may make it necessary for elders to give up their ordinary business in order to devote themselves wholly to the interests of the church, in which case the local brothers should realize their financial responsibility toward them, and seek at least in some measure to make up to them what they have sacrificed for the church's sake (1 Tim. 5:17-18).

(3) For the working brothers and the work. This must be regarded as an offering to God, not as a salary paid to them.

"I robbed other churches, taking wages for the ministry to you. And when I was present with you and lacked, I was not a burden to anyone; for the brothers who came from Macedonia filled up my lack, and in everything I kept myself from being burdensome to you, and will keep myself" (2 Cor. 11:8-9). "And you yourselves also know, Philippians, that in the beginning of the gospel, when I went out from Macedonia, no church had fellowship with me in the account of giving and receiving except you only.... But I have received in full all things and abound; I have been filled, receiving from Epaphroditus the things from you, a sweet-smelling savor, an acceptable sacrifice, well-pleasing to God" (Phil. 4:15, 18). Where the members of a church are spiritual, they cannot but care for the interests of the Lord in places beyond their own locality, and the love of the Lord will constrain them to give both to the workers and to the work. If the members are unspiritual they will probably reason that, since the church and the work are separate, they have no obligations towards the work, and it is enough that they bear responsibility for the church. But those members who are spiritual will always be alive to their responsibility in regard to the work and the workers, and will never seek to evade it on the ground that they have no official responsibility. They will count it both a duty and a delight to further the Lord's interests by their gifts.

While in the Epistles the churches are encouraged to give to the poor saints and also to the local elders and teachers, there is no mention made of encouraging the giving to the apostles, or to the work in which they were engaged. The reason is obvious. The writers of the Epistles were themselves apostles; therefore, it would not have been fitting for them to invite gifts for themselves or their work, nor had they any liberty from the Lord to do so. It was quite in order for them to encourage the believers to give to others, but for the meeting of their own needs and the needs of the work they could only look to God. As they cared for the needs of others, He did not overlook their needs, and He Himself moved the hearts of His saints to supply all that was required. So the workers of today should do as the apostles did of old, concern themselves only with the needs of others, and God will make all their concerns His.

That was a great and noble statement that our brother Paul made to the Philippians. He dared to say to those who were almost his sole supporters, "I have received in full all things and abound." Paul gave no hint of need, but took the position of a wealthy child of a wealthy Father, and he had no fears that by doing so further supplies would not be forthcoming. It was all very well for apostles to say to an unbeliever who himself was in distress, "Silver and gold I do not possess," but it would never have done for a needy apostle to say that to believers who would be ready to respond to an appeal for help. It is a dishonor to the Lord if any representative of His discloses needs that would provoke pity on the part of others. If we have a living faith in God, we shall always make our boast in Him, and we shall dare to proclaim under every circumstance, "I have received in full all things and abound." There is nothing petty or mean about God's true servants; they are all great souls. The following lines were penned by Miss M. E. Barber on Psalm 23:5 when she had used her last dollar:

> There is always something over,
>   When we trust our gracious Lord;
> Every cup He fills o'erfloweth,
>   His great rivers all are broad.
> Nothing narrow, nothing stinted,
>   Ever issued from His store;
> To His own He gives full measure,
>   Running over, evermore.

THE QUESTION OF FINANCE

> There is always something over,
>   When we, from the Father's Hand,
> Take our portion with thanksgiving,
>   Praising for the path He planned.
> Satisfaction, full and deepening,
>   Fills the soul, and lights the eye,
> When the heart has trusted Jesus
>   All its need to satisfy.
>
> There is always something over,
>   When we tell of all His love;
> Unplumbed depths still lie beneath us,
>   Unscaled heights rise far above.
> Human lips can never utter
>   All His wondrous tenderness.
> We can only praise and wonder
>   And His Name for ever bless.

We are the representatives of God in this world, and we are here to prove His faithfulness; therefore, above all in financial matters we must be totally independent of men, and wholly dependent upon God. Our attitude, our words, and our actions must all declare that He alone is our source of supply. If there is any weakness here, He will be robbed of the glory that is His due. As God's servants, we must show forth the abundant resources of our God. We must not be afraid to *appear* wealthy before people. We must never be untrue, but such an attitude is perfectly consistent with honesty. Let us keep our financial needs secret, even if our secrecy should lead men to conclude that we are well off when we have nothing at all. He who sees in secret will take note of all our needs, and He will meet them, not in stinted measure, but "according to His riches, in glory, in Christ Jesus" (Phil. 4:19). We dare to make things difficult for God, because He requires no assistance from us in order to perform His miracles.

From the study of God's Word we note two things concerning the attitude of His children to financial matters. On the one hand, workers should be careful to disclose their needs to none but God; on the other hand, the churches should be faithful in remembering the needs both of the workers and their work, and they should not only send gifts to those who are working in their vicinity, or to those who have been called out from their midst, but, like the Philippians and the Macedonians, they should frequently minister to a far-off Paul. The horizon of the churches should be much wider than it is. The present method of a church supporting its own "minister" or its own missionary was a thing unknown in apostolic days. If, with the present-day facilities for transmitting money to distant parts, the children of God only minister to the material needs of those in their own locality, they certainly lack spiritual insight and largeness of heart. On the part of the workers there must be no expectation from man, and on the part of the churches there should be a faithful remembrance of the work and the workers both at home and abroad. It is essential to the spiritual life of the churches that they take a practical interest in the work. *God has no use for an unbelieving worker, nor has He any use for a loveless church.*

The distinction between the church and the work must be clearly defined in the mind of the worker, especially as regards financial matters. Should a worker pay a short visit to any place on the invitation of the church, then it is quite right for him to receive their hospitality. But should he stay for an indefinite period, then he must bear the burden alone before God; otherwise, his faith in God will wane. Even should a brother willingly offer free hospitality, it ought to be declined, for the life of faith must be carefully maintained. It is right for the brethren to give occasional gifts to the workers, as the Philippians did to Paul, but they must not bear the responsibility of any. The churches have no official obligations regarding the workers, and the latter must see to it that the former do not take such obligations upon themselves. God permits us to accept gifts, but it is not His will that others become responsible for us. Gifts of love may be sent to the workers from their brethren in the Lord, but no believers must regard themselves as under any legal obligations towards them. Not only have the churches no official responsibility towards the workers; they are not even responsible for their board, lodgings, or traveling expenses.

THE QUESTION OF FINANCE

The entire financial responsibility of the work rests upon those to whom it has been committed by God.

"We have wronged no one, we have corrupted no one, we have taken advantage of no one" (2 Cor. 7:2). "I will not be a burden" (2 Cor. 12:14). "For neither were we found at any time with flattering speech, even as you know, nor with a pretext for covetousness; God is witness" (1 Thes. 2:5). "Nor did we eat bread as a gift from anyone, but in labor and hardship we worked night and day so that we would not be burdensome to any of you" (2 Thes. 3:8). From these passages we see clearly the attitude of the apostle. He was not willing to impose any burden upon others or in any way to take advantage of them. And this must be our attitude too. Not only should we receive no salary, we should be careful not to take the slightest advantage of any of our brethren. Apostles should be willing to be taken advantage of, but on no account should they ever take advantage of others. *It is a shameful thing to profess trust in God and yet play the role of a pauper, disclosing one's needs and provoking others to pity.* A servant of God who really sees the glory of God, and his own glorious position as one of His workmen, can well afford to be independent of others, and even liberal. It is only right for us to enjoy the hospitality of our brethren for awhile, but we should most rigidly guard against taking advantage of them in trifles such as a night's lodging, an odd meal, or the use of light and coal, or of household utensils, or even of a daily paper. Nothing reveals smallness of character so readily as taking petty advantages. If we are not careful in such matters, we may as well relinquish our task.

All the movements of workers vitally affect the work, and unless we have a living trust in God, our movements are liable to be determined by prospective incomes. Money has great power to influence men, and unless we have true faith in God and a true heart to do His will, we are likely to be influenced by the rise and fall of funds. If our movements are governed by financial supplies, then we are hirelings working for pay, or beggars seeking alms, and we are a disgrace to the name of the Lord. We should never go to a place because of the bright financial prospects of working there, nor should we refrain from going because the financial outlook is dark. In all our movements we must ask ourselves, Am I in the will of God? or am I influenced at all by financial considerations? We are out to serve the Lord, not to make a living.

THE WORKERS AND THEIR WORK

Let us be clear that we must not only bear the burden of our own personal needs, but of the needs of the work as well. If God has called us to a certain work, then all financial outlay connected with it is our affair. Wherever we go, we are responsible for all expenses relating to it, from its inception to its close. If we are called of God to do pioneering work, though the expenses of rent, furniture, and traveling, may amount to a goodly sum, we alone are responsible for them. He is not worthy to be called God's servant who cannot be responsible for his own needs and the needs of the work to which God has called him. Not the local church, but the one to whom the work has been committed, must bear all financial burdens connected with it.

Another point to which we must give attention is a clear discrimination between gifts intended for personal use and gifts given for the work. It may seem superfluous to mention it, and yet it needs emphasis, that no money given for the work should be used by the worker to meet his personal needs. It must either be used to defray expenses in connection with his own work, or be sent on to another worker. We must learn righteousness in relation to all money matters. If there is any lack in connection with the work, the worker must bear the burden, and if there is any surplus, he cannot divert it to the meeting of his own requirements.

When I had just begun to serve the Lord, I read an incident in Hudson Taylor's life which was a great help to me. If I remember it correctly, this is the gist of it: Mr. Taylor was in St. Louis, U.S.A., and was due in Springfield for meetings. The carriage taking him to the station was delayed, with the result that when he arrived there the train had already left, and there seemed no possible way for him to keep his appointment. But, turning to Dr. J. H. Brookes, he said, "My

Father runs the trains; I'll be there in time." Upon inquiry of the agent, they found a train leaving St. Louis in another direction, which crossed the line going to Springfield; but the train on the other line always left ten minutes before this train arrived, as they were opposing roads. Without a moment's hesitation, Mr. Taylor said he would go that way, in spite of the fact that the agent told him they never made connections there. While they waited, a gentleman came to the station and handed Mr. Taylor some money. He turned to Dr. Brookes with the remark, "Do you not see that my Father has just sent me my train fare!" meaning that, even had he arrived in time for the other train, he could not have taken it. Dr. Brookes was amazed. He knew Mr. Taylor had quite a good sum of money in hand, which had been given him for his work in China, so he asked, "What do you mean by saying you had no money for your fare?" Mr. Taylor replied, "I never use anything for personal expenses that is specified for the work. The money earmarked for my own use has just come in!" For almost the first time in the history of that road the St. Louis train arrived ahead of the other, and Mr. Taylor was able to keep his appointment at Springfield!

MAKING OUR NEEDS KNOWN

As we have already said, an apostle may encourage God's people to remember the needs of the saints and of the elders, but he can mention nothing of his own needs or the needs of the work. Let him only draw the attention of the churches to the wants of others, and God will draw their attention to his wants. Let him be concerned about the needs of the saints and elders, and God will use the saints and elders to draw the attention of the churches to his needs.

We must avoid all propaganda in connection with the work. With utter honesty of heart we must trust in God and make our requirements known to Him alone. Should the Lord so lead, we may tell to His glory what He has wrought through us. (See Acts 14:27; 15:3-4.) But nothing must be done by way of advertisement, in the hope of receiving material help. This is displeasing to God and hurtful to ourselves. If in any financial matter our faith grows weak, we shall find it fail when difficulties arising in connection with the work put it to the test. Besides, if we know anything of the power of the cross to deal with the self-life, how can we resort to propaganda for our work and so take things out of the hands of God and carry them on by our own efforts?

I know of works which, at their inception, were on a pure faith basis, and the blessing of the Lord rested on them. Soon the workers felt the need of extending the work, and actually extended it beyond their usual income. Consequently, they had to resort to indirect advertisement in order to meet their liabilities. Let us beware of extending the work ourselves, for if the extension is of man, we shall have to use man-made methods to meet the new demands. If *God* sees the work needs extension, *He* Himself will extend it, and if *He* extends it, *He* will be responsible to meet the increased needs. It is because human methods are employed to extend a work, that human means must be devised to meet its fresh requirements; so advertisement and propaganda are resorted to in order to solve the problem. Circular letters, reports, magazines, deputation-work, special agents, and special business centers have been means much used of Christian workers to increase funds for the work. Men are not willing to let God extend it in His own time, and because they cannot wait patiently for its spontaneous development, but force an artificial growth, they have to resort to natural activity to meet the demands of that growth. *They* have hastened developments, so *they* have to devise ways and means of procuring increased supplies. The spontaneous growth of the work of God does not necessitate any activities of human nature, for *God* meets all demands which *He* creates.

Advertisement has been developed to a fine art in this age, but if we have to take our cue from businessmen and use up-to-date advertising methods to make our work a success, then let us give up our ministry and change our calling. The wisdom of the world declares that "the end justifies the means," but it is never so in the spiritual realm. Our end must be spiritual, but our means must be spiritual too. The cross is no mere symbol; it is a fact and a principle which must govern all God's work.

We must let the Holy Spirit hinder us where He will, and not seek to urge things forward by touching divine work with human hands. There is no need for us to devise means to draw attention to our work. God in His sovereignty and providence can well bear all responsibility. If *He* moves men to help us, then all is well, but if *we* seek to move men ourselves, both we and the work will suffer loss. If we truly believe God we shall leave the matter wholly in His hands.

We are all trusting God for our living, but what need is there to make it known? I feel repelled when I hear God's servants emphasize the fact that they are living by faith. Do we really believe in God's sovereignty and in His providence? If we do, surely we can trust *Him to make our needs known* to His saints, and so to order things that our needs can be met without our trying to make them known. Even should people conclude from our manner of living that we have a private income, and in consequence withhold their gifts, we do not mind. I would counsel my younger brethren in the ministry not to talk of their personal needs, or of their faith in God, so that they may the better be able to prove Him. The more faith there is, the less talk there will be about it.

AMONG THE FELLOW WORKERS

In the Old Testament we read that though the Levites stood in the place of God to receive tithes from all His people, they themselves offered tithes to Him. The servant of the Lord should learn to give as well as to receive. We praise God for the generous way the workers in days past have given to their fellow laborers, but we still need to be more thoughtful for the material needs of all our brethren in the work. We must remember the words of Paul: "These hands have ministered to my needs and to those who are with me" (Acts 20:34). We must not merely hope to have sufficient to spend on ourselves and our work, but must look to God to provide us with sufficient to give to others too. If we are only occupied with the thought of our personal needs and the needs of our work, and forget the needs of our fellow workers, the plane of our spiritual life is too low. Like Paul, we must constantly think of those with us, and help to minister to their needs. If anyone among us is only a receiver and not a giver, he is unworthy of Him who sent him and those who labor with him.

The scope of our thinking along the line of material needs should always be on the basis of "my needs and to those who are with me." The money God sends to me is not only for me, but also for those with me. A brother once suggested that God would surely supply the needs of all our fellow workers, so we need not feel too concerned about them, especially as we are not a mission and have no financial obligations towards them. But our brother forgot that we are not only responsible for our own needs and the needs of our work, but in a spiritual way we, like Paul, are responsible also for those with us. Whether we are good fellow workers or not will be evidenced by the measure of our thoughtfulness for our brethren in the work.

Since we are not a mission, and have no man-made organization, no headquarters, no centralization of funds, and consequently no distributing center, how can the needs of all our fellow workers be supplied? This question has been repeatedly put to me by interested brethren. The answer is this: all needs will be met if each one realizes his threefold financial responsibility—first, in regard to his personal family and needs; second, in regard to the needs of his work; and third, in regard to the needs of his fellow laborers. We must not only look to God to supply our own wants and all those related to our work, but we must look to Him just as definitely to send us extra funds to enable us to have something to send to our associates in the work. Of course we have no official obligation towards them, but we cannot ignore our spiritual responsibility.

The requirements of workers vary, and the requirements of the work vary too, besides which, the power of prayer differs in different individuals, and the measure of faith differs also. It follows therefore that our income will not be the same; but every one of us should definitely exercise faith for the supply of sufficient funds to be able to distribute to the necessities of others. The amounts we receive and give may differ, but the same principle applies to us all. Working on such a basis, no headquarters is necessary; for each of us acts as a sort of headquarters and distributing center. Of course that does not mean we must send an equal share to all who are associated with us; that is a matter of individual guidance. We trust in the sovereignty and providence of God, and we leave it to Him to regulate the passing on of gifts so that none will have a surplus and none be left in want. Should God lead us to send money regularly to any particular worker, it would be well to send it through one brother this time and another next time, so that the giver will receive less attention from the receiver.

The principle of God's government in relation to financial things is "he who gathered much had no excess, and he who gathered little had no lack" (2 Cor. 8:15). Anyone who has gathered much must be willing to have nothing over, for only then can he who has gathered little have no lack. Some of us have proved in experience that when we bear the burden for those who gather little, God sees to it that we gather much; but if we only think of our own needs, the utmost we can hope for is to gather little and have no lack. It is a privilege to be able to help your brethren in the work, and to be able to give away even the greater proportion of your income. Those who have only learned to take seldom receive; but those who have learned to give are always receiving and have always more to give. The more money you spend on others, the more your income will increase; the more you try to save, the more you will troubled by rust and thieves (Matt. 6:19-20).

We must not confine our giving to those immediately associated with us, but must remember workers in other parts and seek to minister to their needs. We must constantly keep the thought of other workers and their needs before the brethren among whom we labor, and encourage them to help them, never fearing that God will bless other workers more than us. We must leave no room for fear or jealousy. Do we really believe in the sovereignty of God? If so, we shall never fear that anything God has intended for us shall fail to reach us. The needs of Paul and his fellow workers were great, and though he only brought the needs of the saints and the elders before the churches, God looked after his needs and the needs of those with him.

If your work is to be conducted along lines well-pleasing to God, then it is absolutely essential that the sovereignty of God be a working factor in your experience, and no mere theory. When you know His sovereignty, then even if men seem to move around you at random and circumstances appear to whirl at the mercy of chance, you will still be confident in the assurance that God is ordering every detail of your way for His glory and for your good. The needs of others may be known to men, while none may know or even care about your wants, but you will have no anxiety if the sovereignty of God is a reality to you; for then you will see all those haphazard circumstances, and all those indifferent folk, and even the opposing hosts of evil, being silently harnessed to His will; and all those unrelated forces will become related as one to serve His purpose, and to serve the purposes of those whose will is one with His. Yes, "We know that all things work together for good to those who love God, to those who are called according to His purpose" (Rom. 8:28).

So the question is not, Are our needs small or great? or, Are they known or unknown? but simply this, Are we in the will of God? Our faith may be tested, and our patience too, but if we are willing to leave things in God's hands and quietly wait for Him, then we shall not fail to see a careful timing of events and an exquisite dovetailing of circumstances, and emerging from a meaningless maze we shall behold a perfect correspondence between our need and the supply.

WHY NOT A FAITH MISSION?

Some have asked, "Since you believe all God's servants should trust Him for their daily needs, and since you have quite a company of fellow workers, why do you not become an organized faith mission?"

For two reasons: first, in God's Word all association of workers is on a spiritual basis, not on an official one. As soon as you have an official organization, then you change the spiritual relationship which exists among the fellow workers into an official relationship. Second, dependence upon God alone for the meeting of all material needs does not demand as active a faith on the part of an official organization as it does on the part of individuals who are only related in a spiritual fellowship. It is much easier to trust God as a mission than to trust Him as an individual. In Scripture we see individual faith, but we see no such thing as organization-faith. In an organization there is bound to be some income, and every member is sure to receive a share, whether he exercises faith or not. This opens the way for people to join the mission who have no active faith in God. And in the case of those who have faith when they join, there is the likelihood of personal trust in the Lord gradually growing weak through lack of exercise, since supplies come with a certain measure of regularity whether the individual members of the mission exercise faith or not. It is very easy to lose faith in God and simply trust an organization. Those who know the frailty of the flesh realize how prone we are to depend on anything and anyone but God. It is much easier to put our expectation in remittances from the mission than in ravens from heaven. Beloved, is not this the truth? If I have said anything amiss, may God and men both forgive me.

Because of our proneness to look at the bucket and forget the fountain, God has frequently to change His means of supply to keep our eyes fixed on the source. So the heavens that once sent us welcome showers become as brass, the streams that refreshed us are allowed to dry up, and the ravens that brought our daily food visit us no longer; but then God surprises us by meeting our needs through a poor widow, and so we prove the marvelous resources of God. Organization-faith does not stimulate personal trust in God, and that is what He is out to develop.

I know that in an organized body many difficulties vanish automatically. Humanly speaking, it insures a much greater income, for many of God's children prefer to give to organizations rather than to individuals. Besides, organized work comes much more to the notice of the children of God than unorganized. But questions such as these challenge us continually: Do you really believe in God? Must scriptural principles be sacrificed to convenience? Do you really want God's best with all its accompanying difficulties? We do, and so we have no alternative but to work on the ground of the Body of Christ in spiritual association with all others who stand on that same ground.

But we wish to point out that, though we ourselves are not a mission, we are not opposed to missions. Our testimony is positive, not negative. We believe that in God's Word the different groups of sent-out ones who were associated in the work all stood on the ground of the Body, and that no such group was organized into a mission. Still, if our brethren feel led of God to form such an organization, we have nothing to say against it. We only say, God bless them! For us to form a mission because others of God's children do so would be wrong, since we see no scriptural ground for it, and have no leading of the Spirit in that direction. But whether we work in a fellowship whose relationships are only spiritual, or in an organization whose relationships are official, may God make us absolutely one in this, that we do not seek the increase or extension of the companies in which we work, but make it our one aim to work exclusively for the founding and building up of the local churches.

Chapter Nine

THE ORGANIZATION OF LOCAL CHURCHES

Having already observed the difference between the work and the churches, between the apostles and the elders, between the basis of a scriptural church and sects, we can now proceed to see how a local church is organized.

According to the present-day conception, three things are regarded as essential to the existence of a church, apart from the group of Christians who constitute its members. These three are—a "minister," a church building, and "church services." The Christian world would question the existence of a church if even one of these three were lacking.

What would one think these days of a church without a "minister"? Call him pastor or anything else you like, but such a man you certainly must have. As a rule he is specially trained for church work, but he may be either a local man, or a worker transferred from some other place. Whatever his background and qualifications, he gives himself exclusively to the affairs of the church. Thus, those in the churches are divided into two classes—the clergy, who make it their business to attend to spiritual matters, and the laity, who devote themselves to secular things. Then of course there must be church services, for which the minister is responsible, and the most essential of these is the Sunday morning gathering. You may call it a service, or a meeting, or whatever you choose, but such a gathering there must be at least every Sunday, when the church members sit in their pews and listen to the sermon their minister has prepared. And naturally there must be a church building. You may term it a hall, a meeting place, a chapel, or a church; but whatever you care to call it, such a place there must be. Otherwise, how could you ever "go to church" on

Sundays? But what is considered essential to a church these days, was considered totally unnecessary in the early days of the Church's history. Let us see what the Word of God has to say on the matter.

THE "MINISTER," OR WORKER, IN CHURCH GOVERNMENT

"Paul and Timothy, slaves of Christ Jesus, to all the saints in Christ Jesus who are in Philippi, with the overseers and deacons" (Phil. 1:1). In not a single scriptural church do we find any mention of a "minister" controlling its affairs; such a position is always occupied by a group of local elders. And nowhere do we get a clearer or more comprehensive presentation of the personnel of a church than in the verse just quoted from the Philippian letter. The church consists of all the saints, the overseers, and the deacons. The deacons are the men appointed to serve tables (Acts 6:2-6), that is, those who care exclusively for the business side of things. The overseers are the elders, who take the oversight of all church matters. (Acts 20:17, 28, and Titus 1:5, 7 make this quite clear.) And besides the overseers and the deacons, there are all the saints. These three classes comprise the entire church, and no other class of person can be introduced into any church without making it an unscriptural organization.

Before we go on to consider the elders, let us glance for a moment at the deacons. They do not occupy such an important position as the elders, who rule the church; they are chosen by the church to serve it. They are the executors who carry out the decisions of the Holy Spirit through the elders and the church. Because the deacons have actually more to do with assembly life than with the work, we think it sufficient to just make this brief mention of them.

There are two points in connection with the elders that call for special attention. First, they are chosen from among the common *brethren*. They are not workers who have a special call from God to devote themselves exclusively to spiritual work. As a rule they have their families, and their business duties, and are just ordinary believers of good reputation. Second, elders are chosen from among the *local*

THE ORGANIZATION OF LOCAL CHURCHES 165

brethren. They are not transferred from other places, but are set apart just in the place where they live, and they are not called to leave their ordinary occupations, but simply to devote their spare time to the responsibilities of the church. The members of the church are local men, and as elders are chosen from among the ordinary members, it follows that they are also local men (Acts 14:23; Titus 1:5).

And since all scriptural elders are local brothers, if we transfer a man from some other place to control a church, we are departing from scriptural ground. Here again we see the difference between the churches and the work. A brother may be transferred to another place to take care of the work there, but no brother can be sent out of his own locality to bear the burdens of the church in another place. The churches of God are all governed by elders, and elders are *all* chosen from among the local brethren.

If a group of men are saved in a certain place, and a worker is left in charge of them, then it is inaccurate to refer to that company as a church. If affairs are still in the hands of the worker and have not passed into the hands of the local brothers, then it is still his *work;* it is not a *church.* Let us make this distinction clear: the work is always in the hands of the workers, and the church is always in the hands of the local brethren. Whenever a worker is in control of affairs, then it is a question of work, not of a church.

It has been pointed out before that in God's Word there are local elders, but no local apostles. When Paul left Titus in Crete, his object was not that Titus should manage church affairs there, but that he should appoint elders in every place so that *they* could take charge of affairs. The business of the worker is to found churches and appoint elders, never to take direct responsibility in the churches. If in any place an apostle takes responsibility for the affairs of the local church, he either changes the nature of his office or the nature of the church. No apostle coming from another place is qualified for the office of local elder; the post can only be occupied by local men.

Let us who have been called of God to the work be absolutely clear on this point, that we were never called to settle down as pastors in any place. We may revisit the churches we have founded and help the believers we formerly led to the Lord, but we can never become their "minister" and bear the responsibility of spiritual affairs on their behalf. They must be satisfied with the elders appointed by the apostles and learn to honor and obey them. Obviously it needs more grace on the part of the believers to submit themselves to others of their own number and of their own rank, than to yield to the control of a man who comes from another place and has special qualifications for spiritual work. But God has so ordained it, and we bow to His wisdom.

The relationship between the work and the church is really very simple. A worker preaches the gospel, souls are saved, and after a short lapse of time a few of the comparatively advanced ones are chosen from among them to be responsible for local affairs. Thus a church is established! The apostle then follows the leading of the Spirit to another place, and history is repeated there. So the spiritual life and activity of the local church develops, because the believers bear their own responsibility; and the work extends steadily because the apostles are free to move from place to place preaching the gospel and founding new churches.

The first question usually asked in connection with a church is, "Who is the minister?" The thought in the questioner's mind is, "Who is the man responsible for ministering and administering spiritual things in this church?" The clerical system of church management is exceedingly popular, but the whole thought is foreign to Scripture, where we find the responsibility of the church committed to elders, not to "ministers" as such. And the elders only take oversight of the church work; they do not perform it on behalf of the brethren. If, in a company of believers, the minister is active and the church members are all passive, then that company is a mission, not a church. In a church all the members are active. The difference between the elders and the other members is that the latter work, while the former both work themselves *and also* oversee the others as they work. Since the question of elders has been dealt with elsewhere, we shall make no further reference to it here.

THE ORGANIZATION OF LOCAL CHURCHES

THE MEETING PLACE

Another thing which is considered of vital importance to the existence of a church is a church building. The thought of a church is so frequently associated with a church building, that the building itself is often referred to as "the church." But in God's Word it is the living believers who are called the church, not the bricks and mortar (see Acts 5:11; Matt. 18:17). According to Scripture it is not even necessary for a church to have a place definitely set apart for fellowship. The Jews always had their special meeting places, and wherever they went they made a point of building a synagogue in which to worship God. The first apostles were Jews, and the Jewish tendency to build special places of worship was natural to them. Had Christianity required that places be set apart for the specific purpose of worshipping the Lord, the early apostles, with their Jewish background and natural tendencies, would have been ready enough to build them. The amazing thing is that, not only did they not put up special buildings, but they seem to have ignored the whole subject intentionally. It is Judaism, not Christianity, which teaches that there must be sanctified places for divine worship. The temple of the New Testament is not a material edifice; it consists of living persons, all believers in the Lord. Because the New Testament temple is spiritual, the question of meeting places for believers, or places of worship, is one of minor importance. Let us turn to the New Testament and see how the question of meeting places is dealt with there.

When our Lord was on earth, He met with His disciples at times on the hillside and at times by the sea. He gathered them around Him now in a house, again in a boat, and there were times when He drew apart with them in an upper room. But there was no consecrated place, where He habitually met with His own. At Pentecost the disciples were gathered in an upper room, and after Pentecost they either met all together in the temple or separately in different houses (Acts 2:46), or at times in the portico of Solomon (Acts 5.12). They met for prayer in various homes, Mary's being one of them (Acts 12:12), and we read that on a certain occasion they were assembled in a room on the third floor of a building (Acts 20:8). Judging from these passages, the believers assembled in a great variety of places and had no official meeting place. They simply made use of any building that suited their needs, whether a private home, or just a room in a house, or else a large public building such as the temple, or even a wide space like the portico of Solomon. They had no buildings specially set apart for church use; they had nothing which would correspond to the "church" of today.

"And on the first day of the week, when we gathered together to break bread, Paul conversed with them.... And there were a considerable number of lamps in the upper room where we were gathered together. And a certain young man named Eutychus was sitting in the window" (Acts 20:7-9). In Troas we find the believers meeting in the third story of a building. There is a delightfully unofficial air about this gathering, such a contrast to the present-day conventional services, with the church members all sitting stiffly in their pews. But this Troas meeting was a truly scriptural one. There was no official stamp upon it; it bore the marks of real life, in its perfect naturalness and pure simplicity. It was quite all right for some of the saints to sit on the window-ledge, or for others to sit on the floor, as Mary did of old. In our assemblies we must return to the principle of the upper room. The ground floor is a place for business, a place for men to come and go; but there is more of a home atmosphere about the upper room, and the gatherings of God's children are family affairs. The last supper was in an upper room; so was Pentecost, and so again was the meeting here. God wants the intimacy of the upper room to mark the gatherings of His children, not the stiff formality of an imposing public edifice.

That is why in the Word of God we find His children meeting in the family atmosphere of a private home. We read of the church in the house of Prisca and Aquila (Rom. 16:5; 1 Cor. 16:19), the church in the house of Nymphas (Col. 4:15), and the church in the house of Philemon (Philem. 2). The New Testament mentions at least these three different churches that were in the homes of believers. How did churches come to be in such homes? If in a certain place there were a few believers, and one of them had a house large enough to accommodate them all, they quite naturally assembled there, and the Christians in that locality were called "the church in the house of So-and-so."

Everything must begin at the beginning. When a church is founded, the believers from the very outset must learn to meet by themselves, either in their own homes or in some other building which they are able to secure. Of course, not every church is a church in a house, but a church in a house should be encouraged rather than considered as a drawback. If the number of believers is great and the sphere of the locality wide, they might need to meet, as the saints in Jerusalem did, in different houses (which may mean homes, halls, or any other building) instead of in one house. There was only one church in Jerusalem, but its members assembled in different houses. The principle of houses still applies today. This does not mean that the whole church will always meet separately; in fact, *it is important, and of great profit,* for all the believers to gather together quite regularly in one place (1 Cor. 14:23). To make such meetings possible, they could either borrow or rent a public place for the occasion, or, if they have sufficient means, they could acquire a hall permanently for the purpose. But the meeting place for the believers could generally be in a private home. If this is not available, and not suitable, of course other buildings could be acquired. But we should try to encourage meetings in the homes of the Christians.

The grand edifices of today, with their lofty spires, speak of the world and the flesh rather than of the Spirit, and in many ways they are not nearly as well suited to the purpose of Christian assembly as the private homes of God's people. In the first place, people feel much freer to speak of spiritual things in the unconventional atmosphere of a home than in a spacious church building where everything is conducted in a formal manner; besides, there is not the same possibility for mutual intercourse there. Somehow, as soon as people enter those special buildings, they involuntarily settle down to passivity, and wait to be preached to. A family atmosphere should pervade all gatherings of the children of God, so that the brothers even feel free to ask questions (1 Cor. 14:35). Everything should be under the control of the Spirit, but there should be the liberty of the Spirit too. Further, if the churches are in the private homes of the brethren, they naturally feel that all the interests of the church are their interests. There is a sense of closeness of relationship between themselves and the church. Many Christians feel that church affairs are something quite beyond them. They have no intimate concern in them, because in the first place they have their "minister" who is specially responsible for all such affairs, and then they have a great church building which seems so remote from their homes, and where matters are conducted so systematically and with such precision that one feels overpowered and bound in spirit.

Still further, the meetings in believers' homes can be a fruitful testimony to the neighbors around, and they provide an opportunity for witness and gospel preaching. Many who are not willing to go to a "church" will be glad to go to a private house. And the influence is most helpful for the families of the Christians. From early days the children will be surrounded by a spiritual atmosphere, and will have constant opportunity to see the reality of eternal things. Again, if meetings are in the homes of the Christians, the Church is saved much material loss. One of the reasons the Christians survived the Roman persecutions during the first three centuries of Church history, was that they had no special buildings for worship, but met in cellars and caves and other inconspicuous places. Such meeting places were not readily discovered by their persecutors; but the large and costly edifices of today would be easily located and destroyed, and the churches would be speedily wiped out. The imposing structures of our modern times convey an impression of the world rather than of the Christ whose name they bear. *(The halls and other buildings required for the work are quite another matter; we are speaking here only of the churches.)*

So the scriptural method of church organization is simple in the extreme. As soon as there are a few believers in a place, they begin to meet in one of their homes. If numbers increase so that it becomes impracticable to meet in one house, then they can meet in several different houses, but the entire company of believers can meet together once in a while in some public place. A hall for such purposes could either be borrowed, rented, or built, according to the financial condition of the church; but we must remember that the ideal meeting places of the saints are their own private homes.

Meetings connected with the work are arranged along totally different lines, and are entirely under the auspices of the workers. They are on the principle of Paul's own rented house in Rome. As we have seen, when Paul reached Rome a church was already in existence there, and the believers already had their regular gatherings. Paul did not use the meeting place of the church for his work, but rented a separate place, as he stayed for a prolonged period in Rome. In Troas he only stayed for a week, so he did not rent a place there, but simply accepted the hospitality of the church. When he went away, the special meetings he had been conducting there ceased, but the brethren in Troas still continued their own meetings. If a worker intends to remain for a considerable period in any place, then he must obtain a separate center for his work and not make use of the church's meeting place. *Frequently such a center will require more extensive accommodation than the meeting place of the church.* If the Lord calls some of His servants to maintain a permanent testimony in a given place, then the call for a special building in connection with the work may be much greater than the need of premises is in connection with the church. It is almost essential to have a hall if the work is to be carried on in any place, whereas the homes of the brethren will nearly always meet the needs of the church meetings.

THE MEETING

Before we consider the question of meeting, let us first say a few words concerning the nature of the Church. Christ is the Head of the Church and "we who are many are one body in Christ, and individually members one of another" (Rom. 12:5). Apart from Christ, the Church has no head; all believers are only members, and they are "members one of another." Mutuality expresses the nature of the Church, for all the relationships among believers are of one member to another, never of a head to the members. All those who compose a church take their place as members of the Body, not one occupying the position of head. The whole life of the church, and all its activities, must be stamped by this characteristic of mutuality.

But the nature of the work is quite different from that of the church. In the work there are active and passive groups. The apostles are active, and those among whom they labor are passive, whereas in the church all are active. In the work, activity is one-sided; in the church it is all-round.

When we recognize the fundamental difference between the nature of the work and the church, then we shall easily understand the scriptural teaching concerning the meetings which we are about to consider. There are two different kinds of meetings in Scripture—the church meeting and the apostolic meeting. If we are to differentiate clearly between the two, we must first understand the different nature of church and work. Once we see that clearly, a glance at the nature of any meeting will make it obvious to what sphere it belongs; but if we fail to realize the distinction, we shall constantly confuse the church with the work. In the early Church there were meetings which were definitely connected with the churches, and others that were just as definitely connected with the work. In the latter only one man spoke, and all the others constituted his audience. One stood before the others, and by his preaching directed the thoughts and hearts of those who sat quietly listening. This type of meeting can be recognized at once as a meeting connected with the apostolic work, because it bears the character of the work, that is, activity on the one side and passivity on the other. There is no stamp of mutuality about it. In the church meetings, "each one has a psalm, has a teaching, has a revelation, has a tongue, has an interpretation" (1 Cor. 14:26). Here it is not a case of one leading and all the others following, but of each one contributing his share of spiritual helpfulness. True, only a few of those present take part, but all may; only

THE ORGANIZATION OF LOCAL CHURCHES 173

a few are actual contributors to the meeting, but all are potential contributors. The Scriptures show these two distinct kinds of meetings—apostolic meetings, which are led by one man, and church meetings, in which all the local brethren are free to take part.

The apostolic meetings may be divided into two classes— for believers and for unbelievers. The meeting which was held immediately after the Church came into existence was an apostolic meeting for unbelievers (Acts 2:14). The gatherings in the portico of Solomon (Acts 3:11) and in the house of Cornelius (Acts 10) were of the same nature, and there are still other records of similar meetings in the book of Acts. They were clearly apostolic meetings, not church meetings, because one man spoke and all the others listened. Paul's preaching at Troas was to the brethren (Acts 20). Whether it was in the church or not, it was still apostolic in nature, for it was one-sided, the apostle alone speaking to the whole assembly, and not the various members taking part for their mutual edification. Paul preached to the brethren at Troas because he was passing through that place, and any apostle passing through a place as he did would be free to respond to an invitation from the brethren to help them spiritually. Then when Paul was in Rome, the believers came to his rented room to hear him witness (Acts 28:23, 30-31). This work again is specifically apostolic in nature, because one man is active, while the others are passive.

The second kind of meeting is mentioned in the first Epistle to the Corinthians:

> If therefore the whole church comes together in one place, and all speak in tongues, and some unlearned in tongues or unbelievers enter, will they not say that you are insane?... What then, brothers? Whenever you come together, each one has a psalm, has a teaching, has a revelation, has a tongue, has an interpretation. Let all things be done for building up. If anyone speaks in a tongue, it should be by two, or at the most three, and in turn, and one should interpret; but if there is no interpreter, he should be silent in the church, and speak to himself and to God. And as to prophets, two

or three should speak, and the others discern. But if something is revealed to another sitting by, the first should be silent. For you can all prophesy one by one that all may learn and all may be encouraged. And the spirits of prophets are subject to prophets; for God is not a God of confusion but of peace. As in all the churches of the saints (4:23, 26-33).

This is obviously a church meeting, because it is not one man leading while all the others follow, but each gifted one contributing to the meeting as the Spirit directs. In the apostolic meetings there is a definite distinction between the preacher and his audience, but in this kind of meeting any *gifted* member of the church may be preacher and any may be audience. Nothing is determined by man, and each takes part as the Spirit leads. It is not an "all-man" ministry, but a Holy Spirit ministry. The prophets and teachers minister the Word as the Lord gives it, while others minister to the assembly in other ways. Not all can prophesy and teach, but all can seek to prophesy and teach (v. 1). An opportunity is given to each member of the church to help others, and an opportunity is given to each one to be helped. One brother may speak at one stage of the gathering and another later on; you may be chosen of the Spirit to help the brethren this time, and I next time. Everything in the meeting is governed throughout by the principle of "two or three" (vv. 27, 29). Even the same two or three prophets are not permanently appointed to minister to the meetings, but at each meeting the Spirit chooses any two or three from among all the prophets present. That such assemblies are assemblies of the church is seen at a glance, because the stamp of mutuality is clearly upon all the proceedings.

There is only one verse in the New Testament which speaks of the importance of Christians meeting together; it is Hebrews 10:25: "Not abandoning our own assembling together, as the custom with some is, but exhorting one another; and so much the more as you see the day drawing near." This verse shows that the object of such assembling is to exhort "one another." This is obviously not an apostolic meeting, for it is not a case of one man exhorting the entire assembly,

THE ORGANIZATION OF LOCAL CHURCHES 175

but all the members bearing equal responsibility to exhort one another. A church meeting has the stamp of "one another" upon it.

There are several purposes for which the church meets, as recorded in Scripture. First, for prayer (Acts 2:42; 4:24, 31; 12:5); second, for reading (Col. 4:16; 1 Thes. 5:27; Acts 2:42; 15:21, 30-31); third, for the breaking of bread—which are not meetings presided over by a single individual who bears all responsibility, since reference is made to "the cup of blessing which we bless...the bread which we break" (1 Cor. 10:16-17; Acts 2:42; 20:7); and fourth, for the exercise of spiritual gifts (1 Cor. 14). The last type of meeting is a church meeting, for the phrase "in the church" is used repeatedly in the passage which describes it (vv. 28, 34-35). Of this meeting it is said that all may prophesy. How different from one man preaching and all the others sitting quietly in the pew listening to his sermon! That meeting has no place among the different gatherings of the church, for its nature makes it evident that it is an apostolic meeting, and being an apostolic meeting, it belongs to the sphere of the work, not of the church. Meetings where activity is one-sided do not come within the scope of the church, for they lack the distinctive feature of all church gatherings; and where any attempt is made to fit them into the church program, much trouble is sure to result.

Today, alas! this style of meeting is the chief feature of the churches. No meeting is attended with such regularity as this one. Who is considered a really good Christian? Is it not one who comes to church fifty-two Sunday mornings in the year to hear the minister preach? But this is passivity, and it heralds death. Even he who has attended "church" fifty-two Sundays in the year has not really been once to a church meeting. *He has only gone to a meeting in connection with the work.* I do not imply that we should never have this kind of meeting, but the point is that such a meeting is part of the work and is not part of the church. If you have a worker in the locality, then you may have this type of meeting, not otherwise. *The local church, as a church,* has no such meetings. Where they are found in connection with a church, we must discourage them and help believers to see that church meetings are conducted by the church. If apostolic meetings take the place of church meetings, then the church members become passive and indolent, always expecting to be helped, instead of seeking, in dependence upon the Spirit, to be helpful to the other members. It is contrary to the New Testament principles of mutual help and mutual edification. The reason the churches in China are still so weak, after a hundred years of Christian missions, is that God's servants have introduced into the local churches a type of meeting that really belongs to the work, and the church members have naturally concluded that if they attend such services and just passively receive all that is taught them there, they have performed the chief part of their Christian duty. Individual responsibility has been lost sight of, and passivity has hindered the development of spiritual life throughout the churches.

Further, to maintain the Sunday morning preaching, you must have a good preacher. Therefore, a worker is not only needed to manage church affairs, but also to maintain the meetings for spiritual uplift. It is only natural, if a good address is to be delivered *every* Sunday, that the churches hope for someone who is better qualified to preach than recently converted local brothers. How could they be expected to produce a good sermon once a week? And who could be expected to preach better than a specially called servant of God? So an apostle settles down to pastor the church, and consequently the churches and the work both lose their distinctive features. The result is serious loss in both directions. On the one hand, the brethren become lazy and selfish because their thought is only centered on themselves and the help they can receive, and on the other hand, unevangelized territories are left without workers because apostles have settled down to be elders. For lack of activity the spiritual growth of the churches is arrested, and for lack of apostles the extension of the work is arrested too.

Since so much havoc has been wrought by introducing a feature of the work into the churches, and thus robbing both of their true nature, we must differentiate clearly between meetings that belong specifically to the work and those that

THE ORGANIZATION OF LOCAL CHURCHES 177

belong specifically to the church. When God blesses our efforts in any place to the salvation of souls, we must see to it that the saved ones understand, from the outset, that the meetings which resulted in their salvation belong to the work and not to the church, and that *they are the church* and must therefore have *their own* church meetings. They must meet in their homes or in other places to pray, study the Word, break bread, and exercise their spiritual gifts; and in such meetings their object must be mutual helpfulness and mutual edification. Each individual must bear his share of responsibility and pass on to the others what he himself has received from the Lord. The conduct of the meetings should be the burden of no one individual, but all the members should bear the burden together, and they should seek to help one another depending upon the teaching and leading of the Spirit, and depending upon His empowering too. As soon as believers are saved, they should begin to assemble themselves regularly. Such gatherings of local believers are true church meetings.

Meetings connected with the work are only a temporary institution (unless the object is to maintain a special testimony in a special place). But the assembling of the believers for fellowship and mutual encouragement is something permanent. Even should the believers be very immature, and their meetings seem quite childish, they must learn to content themselves with what help they receive from one another and must not always hope to be able to sit down and listen to a good sermon. They should seek revelation, spiritual gifts, and utterance from God; and if their need casts them upon Him, it will result in the enrichment of the whole church. Meetings of recently saved believers will naturally bear the stamp of immaturity at the beginning, but for the worker to take over the responsibility of such meetings will stunt their growth, not foster it. It is the condition of the church meetings, not of the meetings connected with the work, that indicates the spiritual state of a church in any locality. When an apostle is preaching a grand sermon, and all the believers are nodding assent and adding their frequent and fervent "Amens," how deeply spiritual the congregation seems! But it is when they meet by themselves that their true spiritual state comes to light.

The apostolic meeting is not an intrinsic part of the church life; it is merely a piece of work, and it ceases with the departure of the worker. But the church meetings go on uninterrupted, whether the worker is present or absent. It is because the difference has not been realized between meetings for the church and for the work, that it has ever occurred to the brethren to cease to assemble themselves when the worker goes. One of the fruitful sources of spiritual failure today is that the children of God consider the church to be a part of the work; so when there is a sermon to hear, they constitute a willing audience, but if there is no preacher, the meetings automatically cease, and there is no thought of simply gathering together to help one another.

But how can the local believers be equipped to minister one to the other? In the apostolic days it was taken for granted that the Spirit would come upon all believers as soon as they turned to the Lord, and with the on-coming of the Spirit, spiritual gifts were imparted, through the exercise of which the churches were edified. The usual method which God has ordained for building up the churches is the ordinary church gatherings, not the meetings conducted by the workers. The reason the churches are so weak these days is that workers seek to build them up, through the meetings under their care, instead of leaving it to their own responsibility to edify each other through proper church meetings. Why has it come about that the church meetings of 1 Corinthians 14 are no longer a part of church life? Because so many of God's people lack the experience of the Spirit's on-coming, without which a meeting conducted along the lines of 1 Corinthians 14 is *a mere empty form.* Unless all those we lead to the Lord have a definite experience of the Holy Spirit coming upon them, it will be of little use instructing them how to conduct their church meetings, for such meetings will be powerless and ineffective. If the Holy Spirit is upon the believers, as in the days of the early Church, He will give gifts to men, and such men will be able to strengthen the saints and to build up the Body of Christ. We see from Paul's first Corinthian Epistle

THE ORGANIZATION OF LOCAL CHURCHES 179

that God so equipped believers with spiritual gifts that they were able to carry on the work of building up the churches quite independently of the apostles. (This does not imply that they needed no further apostolic help. They decidedly did.) Alas! that nowadays many of God's people set more store by God's servants than by His Holy Spirit! They are content to be ministered to by the gifts of a worker, instead of seeking for themselves the gifts of the Spirit; so true church meetings have given place to meetings under the auspices of the workers.

In 1 Corinthians 14, where a church meeting is in view, apostles have been left out of account altogether! There is *no place* for them in the meetings of a local church! When the members of a church assemble and the spiritual gifts are in use, prophecy and other gifts are exercised, but there is no mention of apostles for the simple reason that apostles are appointed no place in the meetings of the local church; they are appointed to the work. When the local church meets, it is the gifts that are brought into use; office has no place here, not even that of an apostle. But this does not preclude a *visiting* apostle from speaking at all in a church meeting. This is illustrated by the fact that Paul took part in the Troas meeting. But the point to be noted is that Paul was only passing through Troas, so his speaking there was merely a temporary arrangement in order that the local saints might benefit by his spiritual gifts and knowledge of the Lord; it was not a permanent institution.

Apostles, as apostles, represent an office in the work, and not any particular gift; therefore, here they are ignored altogether. Not a mention is made of them in this local church gathering. In the organization of the church they have no place at all, because their ministry, as apostles, was not for the churches but for the work. As we have already observed, apostles had no say in the management of the business affairs of any church; but from the fact that no part is allotted them even in the local gatherings for mutual edification, it is clear that God did not even intend that they should bear the responsibility of the spiritual ministry in the churches. God gave gifts to the local brethren so that they could be prophets, evangelists, shepherds and teachers, and, thus equipped, could carry the burden of spiritual ministry in the locality. Apostles do not bear responsibility either for the spiritual or material side of affairs in any church; the elders are responsible for the local management, and the prophets and other ministers for the local ministry.

Then have apostles nothing to do with the local church? Surely! There is still plenty of scope for them to help the churches, but not in the capacity of apostles. On the business side of things they can help indirectly by giving counsel to the elders, who deal directly with the church affairs; and on the spiritual side in the church meetings they can minister with any spiritual gifts they may possess, such as prophecy or teaching. Their apostolic office is of no account in a church meeting for the exercise of spiritual gifts. As *apostles* they cannot exercise any apostolic gift, but as *brothers* they can minister to their fellow believers by the use of any gift with which the Spirit may have endowed them.

Not only apostles, but even elders as such, have no part in the meetings. In this chapter (1 Cor. 14), elders have no place at all. They are not even mentioned. We have already pointed out that elders are for office, not for ministry. They are appointed for church government, and not for ministry. Office is for government, and gifts are for ministry. In the meetings which are for ministry, it is those who have been gifted by God that count, not those who hold office; so in the church meetings it is the prophets, teachers, and evangelists who take the lead, not the elders. They are the gifted ones of the church.[1]

We must differentiate between the work of the elders, and the work of the prophets and teachers. *Their work is different, but they are not necessarily different persons.* It is quite possible for one person to act in both capacities. The elders are those who hold office in a local church; the prophets and

---

[1] Acts 20:28 ought to be translated, "Take heed to yourselves and to all the flock, among whom the Holy Spirit has placed you as overseers to shepherd the church of God." According to 1 Peter 5:2, this shepherding is by oversight: "Shepherd the flock of God...overseeing."

teachers are the gifted ministers in a local church. The elders are for church government at all times; the prophets and teachers are for ministry *in church meetings*. Whenever there is a church, the Lord not only appoints elders for its government, but also gives gifts to some brothers to constitute them ministers for the meetings. But this does not mean that elders have nothing to do with the meetings. Whenever government in the meetings is necessary, they can exercise authority there. As to ministry, though they cannot minister as elders, yet, if they are also prophets or teachers, they can minister in that capacity. *It is almost imperative that elders be prophets and teachers; otherwise, they cannot rule the church effectively.*

The point to be remembered is that church meetings are the sphere for the ministry of the Word, not the sphere for the exercise of any office. It is for the exercise of gifts unto edification. Since both apostleship and eldership are offices, one in the work and one in the church, so both of the officers, as such, are altogether out of the meetings. But God will be gracious to His church to give it gifts for its upbuilding. The church meetings are the place for the use of these gifts for mutual help.

All meetings on the "round-table" principle are church meetings, and all meetings on the "pulpit-and-pew" principle are meetings belonging to the work. The latter may be of a passing nature, and not necessarily a permanent institution, whereas the former are a regular feature of church life. A round-table enables you to pass something to me and me to pass something to you. It affords opportunity for an expression of mutuality, that essential feature of all relationships in the church. In the local churches we must discourage all meetings on the "pulpit-and-pew" principle, so that, on the one hand, God's workers shall be free to travel far and wide proclaiming the glad tidings to sinners, and, on the other hand, the new converts shall be cast on the Lord for all needed equipment to serve one another. Thus the churches, having to bear their own responsibility, will develop their own spiritual life and gifts through exercise. It is all right to have an apostolic meeting when a worker visits the locality, but when he goes, meetings of the pulpit-type should be discontinued. Prophets, teachers, and evangelists in the local church may also take such meetings from time to time, but they should be regarded as exceptional, for they foster passivity and do not on the whole make for the spiritual development of the churches.

Let us consult the book of Acts in order to see the example God set for His Church in the beginning. "And they continued steadfastly in the teaching and the fellowship of the apostles, in the breaking of bread and the prayers.... And day by day, continuing steadfastly with one accord in the temple and breaking bread from house to house, they partook of their food with exultation and simplicity of heart" (Acts 2:42, 46). Such were conditions in the early days of the Church's history. The apostles did not establish a central meeting place for the believers, but these "continued steadfastly in the teaching and fellowship of the apostles, in the breaking of bread and the prayers." They moved from house to house having fellowship one with another.

We can now draw our own conclusions from the three points we have considered. (1) Wherever there is a group of believers in any place, a few of the more mature are chosen from their number to care for the others, after which all local responsibility rests upon them. From the very outset it should be made clear to the new converts that it is by divine appointment that the management of the church is entrusted to local elders and not to any worker from another place. (2) There is no official meeting place necessary for the church. The members meet in one or more houses, according as their numbers require, and should it be necessary to meet in several houses, it is well for the whole church to congregate from time to time in one place. For such meetings a special place could be obtained either for the occasion, or permanently, according to existing church conditions. (3) The church meetings are not the responsibility of the workers. Local believers should learn to use the spiritual gifts with which God has entrusted them to minister to their fellow believers. The principle on which all church meetings are conducted is that of the "round-table," not of the "pulpit-and-pew." When any apostle visits a place, he could lead a series of meetings for the local church, but such meetings are exceptional. In the usual church gatherings the brethren should all make their special contributions in the power and under the leading of the Spirit. But to make such meetings of definite value it is essential that the believers receive spiritual gifts, revelation, and utterance; therefore, the workers should make it a matter of real concern that all their converts experience the power of the outpoured Spirit.

If the examples God has shown us in His Word are followed, then no question will ever arise in the churches regarding self-government, self-support, and self-propagation. And the churches in the different localities will consequently be saved much unnecessary expenditure, which will enable them to come freely to the help of the poor believers, as the Corinthians did, or to the help of the workers, as did the Philippians. If the churches follow the lines God Himself has laid down for them, His work will go forward unhindered and His kingdom be extended on earth.

THE MINISTRY, THE WORK, AND THE CHURCHES

In the earlier chapters of this book we have already seen what the ministry, the work, and the local churches are. In this chapter we have seen the connection between the ministry and the local church, and also the difference between the church and the work. Now we can consider more minutely the relationship between the ministry, the work, and the churches, in order to see clearly how they stand, how they function, what their respective spheres are, and how they are interrelated.

In Acts 13 we saw that God had established one of His churches in a certain locality; then He gave gifts to a few individuals in that church to equip them to minister there as prophets and teachers, so that the church might be built up. These prophets and teachers constituted the ministry in that church. When in life and in gift these ministers had reached a certain stage of spiritual maturity, God sent two of their number to work in other places; and history repeated itself in the churches established by these two apostles.

Do you not see here the relationship between the churches, the ministry, and the work? (1) God establishes a church in a locality. (2) He raises up gifted men in the church for the ministry. (3) He sends some of these specially equipped men out into the work. (4) These men establish churches in different places. (5) God raises up other gifted men among these churches for the ministry of building them up. (6) Some of these in turn are thrust forth to work in other fields. Thus, the work directly produces the churches, and the churches indirectly produce the work. So the churches and the work progress, moving in an ever-recurring cycle—the work always resulting directly in the founding of churches, and the churches always resulting indirectly in further work.

As to the gifted men raised up of God for the ministry, they labor both in the churches and in the work. When they are in their own locality, they seek to edify the church. When they are in other places, they bear the burden of the work. When they are in the local church, they are prophets and teachers. When they are sent to other places, they are apostles. The men are the same, at home or abroad, but their ministries differ according to the sphere of their service. The prophets and teachers (and shepherds and evangelists), whose sphere is local, plus the apostles, whose sphere is extra-local, constitute the ministry. As the former serve the churches, and the latter the work, the ministry is designed of God to meet the spiritual need in both spheres. Here again we see the relationship between the churches, the ministry, and the work. The work is produced by the churches, the churches are founded as a result of the work, and the ministry serves both the churches and the work.

In Ephesians 4 we see that the sphere of the ministry is the Body of Christ, which may be expressed locally as a church, or extra-locally as the work. It is for this reason also that apostles, prophets, evangelists, and teachers are linked together, though actually the sphere of an apostle's work is quite different from that of the other three. But all belong to the one ministry, whose sphere of service is the Body of Christ. These two groups of men are responsible for the work of the ministry, the one being gifted by the Spirit that they may be enabled to serve the local church, the other called from among these gifted ones to serve Him in different places and given an office in addition to their gifts. Those who have been gifted use their gifts to serve the Church by serving the church in their locality. Those who have both gifts and apostolic commission serve the Church by serving the churches in different localities.

God uses these men to impart His grace to the Church. Their various gifts enable them to transmit grace from the Head to the Body. Spiritual ministry is nothing less than ministering Christ to His people. God's thought in giving these men as a gift to His Church was that a Christ, personally known and experienced by them, might through the gifts of the Spirit, be ministered to His people. They were given to the Church "for the perfecting of the saints unto the work of the ministry, unto the building up of the Body of Christ."

Thus, in the ministry we have the prophets and other ministers using their gifts to serve the local church, while the apostles, by their office and gifts, serve all the churches. The ministry of these two groups of men is of great importance, because all the work of God—local and extralocal—is in their hands. That is why God's Word declares that the Church of God is built upon the foundation of the apostles and prophets.

And in the offices instituted by God, we have the elders occupying the chief place in the local church, while apostles hold no office at all there. Apostles, on the other hand, hold the chief office in the work, while the elders have no place there. Apostles rank foremost in the universal Church, and elders rank foremost in the local church. When we see the distinction between the respective offices of apostles and elders, then we shall understand why the two are constantly linked together (Acts 15:2, 4, 6, 22-23). Apostles and elders are the highest representative of the Church and the churches. Apostles hold the highest office in the work, but in the local church they—as apostles—hold no office at all; elders, on the other hand, hold the chief office in the local church, but as elders they have no place in the work.

And in the local church, there are two departments of service, one relating to business management, the other to spiritual ministry. Offices are connected with the management of the church and are held by the elders and the deacons. Gifts are connected with the ministry of the church and are exercised by the prophets and teachers (and evangelists). The elders and deacons are responsible for the management of the church, while the prophets and teachers concern themselves chiefly with the meetings of the church. Should the deacons and elders also be prophets and teachers, then they could manage church affairs and at the same time, minister to the church in the meetings. We must differentiate between the elders and the ministers. In everyday life, it is the elders who rule the church, but in the meetings for edification, the ministers are the ones ordained by God to serve the church. It should be repeated that elders, *as such,* are appointed for church government, and not for meetings to edify the church. In 1 Corinthians 14, where meetings are in view, elders do not come in at all. But elders, in order to be effective, should also have the gift of a prophet, teacher, shepherd, or evangelist. Yet it must be remembered that when they minister in the meetings they do so, not in the capacity of elders, but as prophets, or teachers, or other ministers. It is in the latter capacity that they have part in the ministry. First Timothy 5:17 makes it clear that the usual sphere of their service is to rule, but some of them (not necessarily all) may also teach and minister.

So the ministry, the work, and the churches are quite different in function and sphere, but they are really coordinated and interrelated. Ephesians 4 speaks of the Body of Christ, but no discrimination is made there between the churches, the work, and the ministry. The saints of the churches, the apostles of the work, and the different ministers of the ministry are all considered in the light of, and in relation to, the Body of Christ. Because whether it be the local church, the ministry, or the work, all are in the Church. They are really one; so while it is necessary to distinguish between them in order to understand them better, we cannot really separate them. Those who are in the different spheres of the Church need to see the reality of the Body of Christ and act relatedly as a body. They should not, because of difference of responsibilities, settle themselves into watertight compartments. "The church, which is His Body," includes the churches, the ministry, and the work. The churches are the Body expressed locally, the ministry is the Body in function, and the work is the Body seeking increase. All three are different manifestations of the one Body, so they are all interdependent and interrelated. None can move, or even exist, by itself. In fact, their relationship is so intimate and vital that none can be right itself without being rightly adjusted to the others. The church cannot go on without receiving the help of the ministry and without giving help to the work; the work cannot exist without the sympathy of the ministry and the backing of the church; and the ministry can only function when there is the church and the work.

This is most important. In the previous chapters we have sought to show their respective functions and spheres; now the danger is lest, failing to understand the spiritual nature of the things of God, we should not only try to *distinguish* between them, but *sever* them into separate units, thus losing the interrelatedness of the Body. However clear the distinction between them, we must remember that they are all in the Church. Consequently, they must move and act as one, for no matter what their specific functions and spheres, they are all in one Body.

So on the one hand, we differentiate between them in order to understand them, and on the other hand, we bear in mind that they are all related as a body. It is not that a few gifted men, recognizing their own ability, take it upon themselves to minister with the gifts they possess; nor that a few persons, conscious of call, form themselves into a working association; nor is it that a number of like-minded believers unite and call themselves a church. All must be on the ground of the Body. The church is the life of the Body in miniature; the ministry is the functioning of the Body in service; the work is the reaching out of the Body in growth. Neither church, ministry, nor work can exist as a thing by itself. Each has to derive its existence from, find its place in, and work for the good of the Body. All three are from the Body, in the Body, and for the Body. If this principle of relatedness to the Body and interrelatedness among its members is not recognized, there can be no church, no ministry, and no work. The importance of this principle cannot be over-emphasized, for without it everything is man-made, not God-created. The basic principle of the ministry is the Body. The basic principle of the work is the Body. The basic principle of the churches is the Body. The Body is the governing law of the life and work of the children of God today.